EDITOR: Maryanne Blacker
FOOD EDITOR: Pamela Clark

∎ ∎ ∎

DEPUTY FOOD EDITOR: Jan Castorina
ASSISTANT FOOD EDITOR: Kathy Snowball
ASSOCIATE FOOD EDITOR: Enid Morrison
SENIOR HOME ECONOMISTS: Alexandra McCowan,
Louise Patniotis, Kathy Wharton
HOME ECONOMISTS: Cynthia Black, Leisel Chen,
Bronwen Clark, Kathy McGarry, Tracey Port,
Maggie Quickenden, Dimitra Stais
EDITORIAL COORDINATOR: Elizabeth Hooper
KITCHEN ASSISTANT: Amy Wong

∎ ∎ ∎

STYLIST: Rosemary de Santis
PHOTOGRAPHER: Robert Clark

∎ ∎ ∎

HOME LIBRARY STAFF:

ASSISTANT EDITOR: Bridget van Tinteren
ART DIRECTOR: Sue de Guingand
DESIGNER: Robbylee Phelan
EDITORIAL COORDINATOR: Fiona Lambrou

∎ ∎ ∎

ACP PUBLISHER: Richard Walsh
ACP DEPUTY PUBLISHER: Nick Chan

∎ ∎ ∎

Produced by The Australian Women's Weekly Home Library.
Typeset by ACP Color Graphics Pty Ltd.
Printed by Times Printers Pte. Ltd, Singapore.
Published by ACP Publishing Pty Ltd, 54 Park Street, Sydney.

◆ USA: Distributed for Whitecap Books Ltd by
Graphic Arts Center Publishing, 3019 N.WYeon,
Portland, OR, 97210. Tel: 503-226-2402. Fax: 530-223-1410.

◆ CANADA: Distributed in Canada by Whitecap
Books Ltd, 1086 West 3rd St,
North Vancouver B.C. V7P 3J6.
Tel: 604-980-9852. Fax: 604-980-8197.

∎ ∎ ∎

Beginners' Cookbook

Includes index.
ISBN 0 86396 003 1

© ACP Publishing Pty Limited 1994
ACN 053 273 546
This publication is copyright. No part of it may be reproduced
or transmitted in any form without the written permission
of the publishers.

∎ ∎ ∎

COVER: Chicken, Bean and Tomato
Casserole, page 74.
OPPOSITE: Racks of Lamb with Red Currant
Port Glaze, Baked Sweet Potato Crescents, Peas
with Garlic and Bacon, page 10.
BACK COVER: Honey and Garlic Shrimp Kabobs, page 6.
INSIDE BACK COVER: Salad Nicoise, page 54.

BEGINNERS COOKBOOK

You can start with any recipe in this book, and cook a great meal even if you have never cooked before. First, take time to read the recipes, check the important points and photographs, then organise your shopping. We did not use salt and pepper for seasoning, but you can add them, if you prefer. It is important to refrigerate fresh produce soon after purchase, and always handle hot foods with care. Also check our big reference section at the back of this book for further guidance. Although we had no space for microwave instructions, follow your microwave oven manual for guidelines with similar foods. It's as easy as that to start cooking with our friendly, expert help!

Pamela Clark

FOOD EDITOR

■ NACHOS WITH GUACAMOLE
■ CABBAGE AND CUCUMBER SALAD

Mexico's famous chili bean and tomato dip is wonderful with creamy avocado, all scooped up with crunchy corn chips and accompanied by fresh cabbage salad with lime dressing. Serves 4.

SHOPPING LIST

¼ small (about 10oz) savoy cabbage
½ medium avocado
1 small (about 6oz) green cucumber
fresh cilantro
1 medium (about 5oz) onion
1 small (about 2½oz) onion
1 lime
1 lemon
garlic
8¾oz can red kidney beans
14½oz can whole peeled tomatoes
3½oz cheddar cheese
1½oz cheese-flavored corn chips
sour cream
light olive and salad oils
chili powder
paprika
sugar

WORK PLAN

1 Prepare salad vegetables and lime dressing.

2 Mash beans and chop onions.

3 Cook chili bean mixture.

4 Prepare guacamole.

5 Assemble chili bean mixture, corn chips and cheese in dish and bake.

6 Toss salad with lime dressing.

7 Top nachos with guacamole and sour cream and serve with cabbage and cucumber salad.

NACHOS WITH GUACAMOLE

Important Points

● Chili powder varies in strength, so use more or less, depending on your taste.

● Choose a bruise-free avocado. Test for ripeness by gently pressing around neck which should yield softly. Store at room temperature until fully ripe, then store in the refrigerator for up to 3 days. To peel avocado, see Techniques section.

● Guacamole must be made just before serving; it can be served on its own, with corn chips, as a snack.

● Chili bean mixture can be prepared a day ahead, cooled and stored, covered, in the refrigerator.

● Chili bean mixture suitable to freeze.

● Recipe not suitable to microwave.

You Need

8³⁄₄oz can red kidney beans
14¹⁄₂oz can whole peeled tomatoes
1 medium (about 5oz) onion
1 tablespoon light olive oil
1 clove garlic, minced
¹⁄₄ teaspoon chili powder

¹⁄₄ teaspoon paprika
¹⁄₂ teaspoon sugar
¹⁄₃ cup water
1¹⁄₂oz cheese-flavored corn chips
³⁄₄ cup grated cheddar cheese
3 tablespoons sour cream

1 Place beans in a strainer, rinse under cold water; drain well. Place undrained tomatoes into a medium bowl and mash with a fork or potato masher. Chop onion finely.

2 Heat oil in a medium skillet, add onion and garlic, cook, stirring, over low heat until onion is soft but not colored. Add chili powder and paprika, stir over heat for 1 minute to remove the raw taste of the spices.

3 Mash beans in a medium bowl with a fork or potato masher. Add mashed tomatoes and beans, sugar and water to the skillet. Bring mixture to the boil, reduce heat, simmer, uncovered, stirring occasionally, for about 20 minutes or until mixture is thickened.

4 Spoon chili bean mixture into a lightly greased ovenproof dish (3 cup capacity). Place corn chips around edge of dish, sprinkle with cheese. Bake, uncovered, in 375˚F oven for about 5 minutes or until cheese is melted. Remove from oven. Serve nachos topped with guacamole and sour cream.

GUACAMOLE

You Need

½ medium avocado
½ small onion

4 teaspoons sour cream
2 teaspoons fresh lemon juice

1 Peel and chop the avocado. Place avocado in a small bowl and mash with a fork until smooth (or process avocado until smooth). Chop onion finely.

2 Add onion, sour cream and lemon juice to avocado in the bowl; mix well.

CABBAGE AND CUCUMBER SALAD

Important Points

- Choose cabbage without marks and insect holes. Cut away hard core and discard outer leaves before use.
- Store cabbage for up to 2 weeks in the vegetable crisper in the refrigerator, covered in plastic wrap.
- Choose a firm, bright green cucumber. Store in the vegetable crisper in the refrigerator.
- Salad can be prepared a day ahead and stored, covered, in the refrigerator.
- Not suitable to freeze.

You Need

¼ small (about 10oz) savoy cabbage
½ small onion
1 small (about 6oz) green cucumber
2 teaspoons chopped fresh cilantro

Lime Dressing
¼ cup salad oil
1 tablespoon fresh lime juice
1 clove garlic, minced

1 Shred cabbage finely. Chop onion finely. Peel cucumber, slice in half lengthways. Remove seeds using a teaspoon. Slice cucumber thinly. Combine all ingredients in a large bowl, add dressing; mix well.

2 Lime Dressing: Combine oil, lime juice and garlic in a small bowl, mix well with a wire whisk (or combine all ingredients in a screw-top jar; shake well).

■ HONEY AND GARLIC SHRIMP KABOBS

■ JULIENNE OF VEGETABLES

We show you how to peel shrimp the easy way, then how to transform them into smart little kabobs and broil them. For the vegetables, "julienne" means cutting vegetables into fine sticks. Serves 4.

SHOPPING LIST

36 (about 2lb) uncooked jumbo shrimp
2 medium (about ½lb) carrots
2 medium (about 7oz) zucchini
1 medium (about ¾lb) leek
garlic
1 lemon
fresh chives
light soy sauce
hoisin sauce
barbeque sauce
chili sauce
honey
light olive oil
butter

WORK PLAN

1 Shell and devein shrimp.

2 Prepare marinade.

3 Marinate shrimp.

4 Prepare vegetables.

5 Place shrimp on skewers.

6 Preheat broiler.

7 Broil shrimp.

8 Stir-fry vegetables.

9 Serve honey and garlic shrimp kabobs immediately with julienne of vegetables.

HONEY AND GARLIC SHRIMP KABOBS

Important Points

- Shrimp are available all year round. Uncooked shrimp are often known as "green".
- Shells should be firmly intact and have a pleasant sea smell; they should not be sweaty or have any discoloration.
- When cooked, the shells turn orange-red.
- If buying cooked shrimp for another dish, look for firm flesh with a tight shell, and a good color.
- Store cooked or uncooked shrimp, unshelled, in an airtight container. Refrigerate for up to 2 days, depending on freshness when purchased.
- Use stainless steel or wooden skewers. Stainless steel are unsuitable for use in the microwave oven, but are ideal for barbequeing, broiling or frying. The advantage is that you can use, wash and use them again.
- Soak wooden skewers for at least 1 hour or overnight to help minimise burning during cooking. Dispose of skewers after use.
- Shrimp can be prepared 2 hours ahead and stored, covered, in the refrigerator.
- Serve honey and garlic shrimp kabobs with herbed rice, if desired; see page 99.
- Not suitable to freeze.
- Not suitable to microwave.

You Need

36 (about 2lb) uncooked jumbo shrimp
3 tablespoons light soy sauce
1 tablespoon hoisin sauce
4 teaspoons barbeque sauce

1 teaspoon chili sauce
4 teaspoons honey
3 tablespoons light olive oil
3 cloves garlic, minced

1 Pinch head from body of shrimp, pinch tail section away, then peel shell away from center area. If you want to keep tail intact, leave tail and next section of shell in place, and pull away center shell. Run a knife lightly down the center back of the shrimp; do not cut right through. Remove the black thread or vein that runs along the center of the shrimp. This instruction can be abbreviated as "shell and devein shrimp".

2 Combine soy sauce, hoisin sauce, barbeque sauce, chili sauce, honey, oil and garlic in large bowl; mix well. Add shrimp, stir to coat shrimp well with marinade, cover, refrigerate for 2 hours.

3 Remove shrimp from marinade, reserve marinade. Thread shrimp onto 12 metal or wooden skewers.

4 Preheat broiler. Cover a wire rack with foil, place kabobs on rack, broil under high heat until shrimp have changed in color. Turn shrimp, brush with reserved marinade. Broil until changed in color and tender.

JULIENNE OF VEGETABLES

Important Points

● Julienne of vegetables are thin strips or matchsticks of almost any vegetable. We have used carrots, zucchini and leek here; you could also use red or green bell peppers, asparagus, beans or eggplant, just to mention a few.

● Try to cut strips as evenly as possible; this takes care, practice and patience. Use a good sharp knife.

● Choose fresh, firm vegetables of uniform size, if possible.

● If preparing vegetables for julienne ahead of time, keep covered in plastic wrap in the refrigerator, not soaking in water, which can make them lose flavor.

● Serve julienne of vegetables immediately.

● Not suitable to freeze.

● Suitable to microwave.

You Need

2 medium (about ½lb) carrots
2 medium (about 7oz) zucchini
1 medium (about ¾lb) leek

2 tablespoons (¼ stick) butter
2 teaspoons chopped fresh chives
4 teaspoons fresh lemon juice

1 Peel carrots. Trim about ½ inch from ends of the zucchini. Slice carrots and zucchini thinly lengthways. Stack the slices on top of each other, and slice again into thin strips. Using only the white part of the leek, cut leek in half lengthways; wash away grit; see Techniques section. Open leek out flat and slice into thin strips.

2 Heat butter in a large skillet or wok, add vegetables, stir-fry over high heat for about 2 minutes or until just tender, stir in chives and juice.

RACKS OF LAMB WITH RED CURRANT PORT GLAZE

Important Points

- Lamb is at its best during spring. Store in the meat keeper or in the coldest part of the refrigerator on a plate or on a rack over a plate, loosely covered with baking paper, then plastic wrap or foil, allowing air to circulate around the meat.

- Racks of lamb are simply chops joined together. You can ask your butcher to cut a rack consisting of 2 chops or as many chops as you require.

- Allow 2 to 4 chops per person depending on the size of the chops, and individual appetites.

- Scrape excess meat and fat from bones with a sharp knife so bones won't burn during cooking or have the butcher "French" the bones for you.

- Do not season meat for roasting with salt, as this tends to draw out the meat's juices.

- Cooking times will vary depending on how thick or how large the chops are, and also on your personal taste; 30 minutes will generally give you slightly pink lamb, but you can cook for up to 45 minutes, if preferred.

- Racks of lamb can be served whole or sliced into chops.

- For chicken broth for the glaze, see page 121.

- Stand racks of lamb, covered, in a warm place for 5 minutes before serving.

- Not suitable to freeze.

- Not suitable to microwave.

You Need

4 racks of lamb (3 chops each)
ground black pepper

Red Currant Port Glaze

1 small (about 2½oz) onion
4 teaspoons chopped fresh rosemary
3 tablespoons fresh orange juice
½ cup port wine
¼ cup chicken broth
3 tablespoons red currant jelly
1 teaspoon cornstarch
1 teaspoon water

1 With a knife, trim as much excess fat as possible from lamb and scrape away excess meat for about 1½ inches from ends of bones. Sprinkle lamb with pepper, place lamb on a wire rack in a roasting pan. Bake, uncovered, in 350°F oven about 30 minutes or until lamb is cooked as desired. Remove lamb from wire rack to plate, cover with foil, stand for 5 minutes before serving. Reserve any juices in the roasting pan for red currant port glaze.

2 Red Currant Port Glaze: Chop onion finely. Pour any reserved juices from roasting pan and plate into a medium skillet, add onion, cook, stirring, over medium heat until onion is soft. Add rosemary, orange juice, port wine, broth and jelly, stir over heat until jelly is melted. Bring to the boil, reduce heat, simmer, uncovered, until mixture is reduced by about half. Blend cornstarch and water in small bowl with a teaspoon, stir into red currant mixture, stir constantly over heat until glaze boils and thickens. Strain before serving.

BAKED SWEET POTATO CRESCENTS

Important Points

- Not suitable to freeze.
- Not suitable to microwave.

You Need

2 small (about 1lb) sweet potatoes
all-purpose flour
3 tablespoons butter

½ teaspoon paprika
½ teaspoon celery salt
½ teaspoon dried oregano leaves

1 Peel potatoes, cut into ½ inch slices, cut slices in half. Toss crescents in flour, shake away excess flour. Place in a single layer on lightly greased baking sheet.

2 Melt butter in small saucepan, stir in paprika, salt and oregano. Brush mixture over potato, bake, uncovered, in 350°F oven about 45 minutes or until soft.

PEAS WITH GARLIC AND BACON

Important Points

- Not suitable to freeze.
- Suitable to microwave.

You Need

1lb fresh green peas
2 slices bacon
2 cloves garlic, minced

1 Half fill a pan with water, bring to boil, add shelled peas, return to the boil, simmer, uncovered, until tender. Drain, rinse under cold water; drain.

2 Remove rind from bacon, chop bacon. Place bacon in skillet, stir over heat until crisp. Reduce heat, add garlic and peas, stir until hot.

■ LEMON CHICKEN PARCELS
■ NEW POTATOES
■ FRESH ASPARAGUS

Lightly fried boneless, skinless chicken breast halves are first spread with a little seeded mustard and cilantro, and encased in packaged phyllo pastry. Keep pastry covered with plastic wrap, then a well-wrung-out, damp kitchen towel to prevent it from drying and crumbling while using it. Serves 4.

SHOPPING LIST

4 boneless, skinless chicken breast halves
phyllo pastry
heavy cream
16 (about 1¼lb) baby new potatoes
2 bunches (about 1lb) fresh asparagus
fresh gingerroot
fresh cilantro
fresh chives
1 lemon
butter
light olive oil
seeded mustard

WORK PLAN

1 Brown chicken; cool.

2 Prepare chicken parcels.

3 Put water on for potatoes.

4 Put chicken in oven.

5 Cook potatoes.

6 Put water on for asparagus.

7 Make sauce for chicken.

8 Cook asparagus.

9 Drain potatoes, toss in butter and chives.

10 Drain asparagus.

11 Serve lemon chicken parcels immediately with new potatoes and fresh asparagus.

15

LEMON CHICKEN PARCELS

Important Points

- Fresh uncooked chicken should be stored in the meat keeper or in the coldest part of the refrigerator on a plate or on a rack over a plate, loosely covered with plastic wrap or foil.
- Chicken parcels can be prepared 3 hours ahead and stored, covered, in the refrigerator.
- Uncooked chicken parcels suitable to freeze. Sauce not suitable to freeze.
- Chicken parcels not suitable to microwave. Sauce suitable to microwave.

You Need

4 boneless, skinless chicken breast halves
2 tablespoons (¼ stick) butter
1 tablespoon light olive oil
8 sheets phyllo pastry
¼ cup (½ stick) butter, melted, extra
4 teaspoons seeded mustard
4 teaspoons chopped fresh cilantro

Sauce

4 teaspoons fresh lemon juice
4 teaspoons chopped fresh cilantro
4 teaspoons grated fresh gingerroot
½ cup heavy cream

1 Trim away excess fat from chicken. Heat butter and oil in a medium skillet, add chicken, cook on both sides until lightly browned. Remove chicken from the skillet, drain on absorbent paper; cool. Reserve the skillet with juices for sauce.

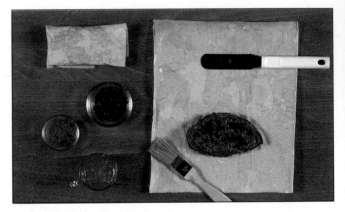

2 Place 1 sheet of pastry on bench, brush with extra butter. Top with another layer of pastry, brush with butter. Fold pastry in half, place a chicken piece in center of 1 end of pastry. Spread chicken with some of the mustard and sprinkle with a little cilantro. Fold sides of pastry over chicken, roll up to form a parcel. Repeat with remaining pastry, butter, chicken, mustard and cilantro.

3 Place chicken parcels on baking sheet, brush parcels with remaining extra butter. Bake, uncovered, in 350°F oven about 20 minutes or until golden brown. Pierce with a skewer, chicken is cooked when juices run clear.

4 Sauce: Add lemon juice to the reserved juices in the skillet, stir in cilantro, gingerroot and cream. Simmer, stirring constantly, over heat until reduced by half and slightly thickened. Serve sauce over chicken parcels.

NEW POTATOES

Important Points

- Not suitable to freeze.
- Suitable to microwave.

You Need

16 (about 1¼lb) baby new potatoes
3 tablespoons butter

4 teaspoons chopped fresh chives

1 Place washed potatoes in a medium saucepan, cover with cold water; cover, bring to boil, reduce heat, simmer until potatoes are tender; drain.

2 Heat butter in same saucepan, return potatoes to the pan, stir to coat potatoes with butter, sprinkle potatoes with chives.

FRESH ASPARAGUS

Important Points

- Asparagus spears are very perishable. Store, without washing, in the vegetable crisper, or in a plastic bag wrapped in a sheet of absorbent paper, in the refrigerator. Store for 2 to 3 days only.
- Not suitable to freeze.
- Suitable to microwave.

You Need

2 bunches (about 1lb) fresh asparagus spears

1 Break off coarse ends of spears; see Techniques section. Scrape nodules from the ends of the spears (not the tips), using a vegetable peeler.

2 Half fill a medium saucepan with water. Bring water to boil, add spears, return to boil, simmer, uncovered, about 2 minutes or until just tender (test with knife); drain.

MINESTRONE WITH MEATBALLS
GARLIC BREAD

A thick, substantial soup of Italian origin, minestrone means "the first big course". It usually contains mixed vegetables in season, plus pasta, rice, beans or potatoes, but there are many versions from different regions of Italy. We have used canned beans for convenience, and added mini meatballs to make it even more of a meal; you can omit the meatballs, if you like. The crusty garlic bread is a quick and tasty accompaniment. Serves 6.

SHOPPING LIST

2 medium (about 10oz) onions
1 medium (about ¼lb) carrot
1 stalk celery
fresh basil
fresh chives
garlic
1lb ground beef
14½ oz can whole peeled tomatoes
10oz can three-bean mix
3½oz spaghetti pasta
fresh bread crumbs
butter
light olive oil
egg
Parmesan cheese
chicken broth
small French bread stick

WORK PLAN

1 Prepare garlic bread and refrigerate.

2 Prepare meatballs; cook meatballs.

3 Prepare vegetables for soup.

4 Put soup on to cook.

5 Add pasta and meatballs to soup.

6 Heat garlic bread.

7 Serve minestrone with meatballs and garlic bread.

MINESTRONE WITH MEATBALLS

Important Points

- There are many recipes for minestrone; we used canned beans for convenience, but you can use any mix of dried beans; ⅔ cup (¼lb) dried beans equals approximately the amount in a 10oz can. Place dried beans in a large bowl, cover well with water, cover, stand overnight. Drain beans, place beans in a large pan, cover with water, bring to the boil, simmer, covered, for about 30 minutes or until tender; drain.
- Store ground beef in the meat keeper or in the coldest part of the refrigerator on a plate, loosely covered with plastic wrap or foil, allowing air to circulate around beef. Use within 2 days of purchase.
- Meatballs can also be served on their own or with a sauce; see tomato sauce on page 34.
- Recipe can be made a day ahead and stored, covered, in the refrigerator.
- Suitable to freeze.
- Not suitable to microwave.

You Need

1 medium (about 5oz) onion
1 stalk celery
1 medium (about ¼lb) carrot
14½oz can whole peeled tomatoes
10oz can three-bean mix
4 teaspoons light olive oil

1 clove garlic, minced
6 cups chicken broth
3½oz spaghetti pasta
4 teaspoons chopped fresh basil
¼ cup grated Parmesan cheese

1 Chop onion, celery and carrot finely. Pour undrained tomatoes into a medium bowl, crush with a fork or potato masher. Drain beans in a strainer, rinse under cold water; drain well.

2 Heat oil in a large saucepan, add celery, carrot, onion, and garlic, cook, stirring, over medium heat for about 3 minutes or until onion is soft.

3 Add undrained crushed tomatoes, beans and broth (see page 121) to the saucepan, bring to the boil, simmer, covered, for 15 minutes.

4 Add pasta and meatballs to the saucepan, simmer, uncovered, for about 15 minutes or until pasta is tender; stir in basil. Serve minestrone sprinkled with cheese.

MEATBALLS

You Need

1 medium (about 5oz) onion
1lb ground beef
¾ cup fresh bread crumbs

2 cloves garlic, minced
1 egg yolk
3 tablespoons light olive oil

1 Chop onion finely. Combine onion, beef, bread crumbs, garlic and egg yolk in a large bowl; mix well (or process all ingredients in a food processor until finely ground).

2 Roll 2 level teaspoons of mixture into a ball. Repeat with remaining mixture. Heat oil in a large skillet, add meatballs, cook over medium heat, turning occasionally, until cooked through; drain.

GARLIC BREAD

Important Points

● Garlic and chives can be stirred into softened butter and spread on the cut slices of bread as an alternative.
● Garlic bread can be prepared for cooking 3 hours ahead and stored, well wrapped in foil, in the refrigerator.
● Uncooked buttered bread suitable to freeze.
● Not suitable to microwave.

You Need

1 small French bread stick
¼ cup (½ stick) butter

1 clove garlic, minced
2 teaspoons chopped fresh chives

1 Slice bread stick diagonally with a serrated knife, cutting almost to the base but not right through. Melt butter in a small saucepan, stir in garlic and chives.

2 Gently pull slices apart and brush a little garlic butter between each pair of slices. Brush top of bread stick with remaining butter, wrap in foil, place in 350°F oven for about 10 minutes or until heated through.
Uncover bread stick, return to oven, cook for 5 minutes.

■ BROILED FISH WITH TARTARE SAUCE
■ SNOW PEAS WITH ALMONDS
■ SAUTE POTATOES

It's very quick to broil fish to your taste, and serve with tartare sauce, the traditional accompaniment. We've added buttered snow peas with toasted almonds, and crispy, chunky potatoes. Serves 4.

SHOPPING LIST

4 medium (about 1¼lb) white fish cutlets
7oz snow peas
4 medium (about 1¼lb) potatoes
fresh rosemary
fresh parsley
1 lemon
light olive oil
butter
sliced almonds
dill pickle
capers
mayonnaise
Worcestershire sauce

WORK PLAN

1 Prepare tartare sauce, cover, refrigerate.

2 Peel and boil potatoes.

3 Toast almonds.

4 Trim tops from snow peas, remove strings.

5 Saute potatoes slowly.

6 Preheat broiler.

7 Put water on for snow peas.

8 Broil fish.

9 Cook and drain snow peas.

10 Turn fish.

11 Toss snow peas in butter and nuts.

12 Serve broiled fish with tartare sauce, snow peas with almonds and saute potatoes.

23

BROILED FISH WITH TARTARE SAUCE

Important Points

● Fish should be eaten as soon as possible after purchase. If not eaten immediately, fish should be wrapped in plastic wrap and stored in an airtight container in the coldest part of the refrigerator for up to 2 days.

● When choosing fish, feel the fish, if possible; the flesh should feel firm to touch. Fish should not smell unpleasant.

● Most cuts of fish are suitable for broiling; for example, cutlets, fillets, steaks and whole fish. Cooking times will vary.

● Serve fish immediately as it will become tough and dry if reheated or kept hot for any length of time. Tartare sauce can be made a day ahead and stored, covered, in the refrigerator.

● Not suitable to freeze.

● Not suitable to microwave.

You Need

4 medium (about 1¼lb) white fish cutlets
1 tablespoon oil or melted butter

Tartare Sauce

1 large dill pickle
4 teaspoons capers
½ cup mayonnaise
2 teaspoons chopped fresh parsley
½ teaspoon fresh lemon juice
½ teaspoon Worcestershire sauce

1 Preheat broiler. Place fish cutlets slightly apart on greased foil on a broiler tray. Brush fish lightly with some of the oil or melted butter.

2 Broil fish under high heat for 3 minutes. Turn fish carefully with tongs, brush with a little more oil or butter. Broil fish for 3 more minutes or until fish flakes easily when tested with a fork.

3 Tartare Sauce: Chop dill pickle finely. Drain capers in a small strainer, chop finely.

4 Place mayonnaise in a medium bowl, add dill pickle, capers, parsley, lemon juice and Worcestershire sauce; stir until well combined, cover, refrigerate.

SNOW PEAS WITH ALMONDS

Important Points

● Not suitable to freeze.
● Snow peas suitable to microwave.

You Need

3 tablespoons sliced almonds
7oz snow peas
1 tablespoon butter

1 Preheat broiler. Place almonds on a baking sheet, toast under broiler until lightly browned; set aside. Trim tops from snow peas and remove strings.

2 Add snow peas to boiling water, simmer, uncovered, for 30 seconds; drain, rinse under cold water, drain. Return to saucepan, add butter and almonds, reheat.

SAUTE POTATOES

Important Point

● Potatoes can be boiled in the microwave oven.

You Need

4 medium (about 1¼lb) potatoes
3 tablespoons butter

3 tablespoons light olive oil
4 teaspoons chopped fresh rosemary

1 Peel and chop potatoes, place in a medium saucepan, cover with cold water. Cover saucepan with lid, bring to the boil, simmer until potatoes are just tender; drain.

2 Heat butter and oil in a large skillet, add potatoes, saute over medium heat, stirring occasionally, until browned and crisp. Sprinkle with rosemary.

■ HEARTY VEGETABLE CURRY WITH PAPPADAMS
■ TOMATO, MINT AND LIME SALAD
■ YOGURT WITH CUCUMBER
■ NUTTY RICE

We have made a quick and easy curry using prepared curry powder instead of mixing spices in the traditional manner; instead of fresh vegetables, you can use leftover cooked vegetables, if you prefer. It's accompanied by spicy steamed rice. The side dishes, known as sambals, are a minted tomato salad and yogurt with cucumber. Serves 4.

SHOPPING LIST

2 large (about ¾lb) carrots
2 large (about 14oz) potatoes
1 medium (about ½lb) parsnip
1 medium (about 5oz) onion
5oz broccoli
¼ medium (about ½lb) cauliflower
5oz button mushrooms
2 medium (about ½lb) tomatoes
1 medium lime
1 small (about 6oz) green cucumber
5 green onions
fresh gingerroot
fresh mint
garlic
1 lemon
1⅔ cups canned unsweetened coconut milk
ghee
12 small pappadams
plain yogurt
golden raisins
roasted unsalted cashews
cinnamon stick
coriander seeds
cardamom pods
cuminseed
curry powder
chili powder
oil
sugar
rice
coarse (kosher) salt

WORK PLAN

1 Peel and salt cucumber.

2 Wash rice and drain.

3 Prepare vegetables for curry.

4 Put curry on to cook.

5 Put rice on to cook.

6 Rinse cucumber and prepare yogurt with cucumber.

7 Prepare tomato, mint and lime salad.

8 Finish off rice.

9 Cook pappadams.

10 Serve curry with pappadams, tomato, mint and lime salad, yogurt with cucumber and nutty rice.

HEARTY VEGETABLE CURRY WITH PAPPADAMS

Important Points

- This curry is a good way of using leftover vegetables. Only trial and error will help you find the curry powder you like best, and the amount to use of that powder. Keep curry powder in an airtight container away from the light.
- We have shallow-fried our pappadams. They can also be cooked in the microwave oven without any oil. Place 4 small pappadams in the microwave oven, cook on HIGH (100 percent) until pappadams are puffed evenly.
- Pappadams are best cooked just before serving.
- Hearty vegetable curry can be cooked a day ahead, cooled and stored, covered, in the refrigerator.
- Not suitable to freeze.
- Suitable to microwave.

You Need

2 large (about ¾lb) carrots
2 large (about 14oz) potatoes
1 medium (about ½lb) parsnip
1 medium (about 5oz) onion
5oz broccoli
¼ medium (about ½lb) cauliflower
5oz button mushrooms
2oz ghee

2 cloves garlic, minced
4 teaspoons curry powder
2 teaspoons grated fresh gingerroot
1⅔ cups canned unsweetened coconut milk
1 cup water
1 cup oil for shallow-frying
12 small pappadams

1 Prepare vegetables. Peel and cut carrots, potatoes and parsnip into 1¼ inch pieces. Chop onion. Break broccoli and cauliflower into small florets and chop stems. Wipe mushrooms, cut in half.

2 Heat ghee in a large saucepan, add onion, garlic, curry powder and gingerroot. Cook, stirring, over low heat until onion is soft and curry powder is fragrant.

3 Add carrots and coconut milk, stir until boiling, reduce heat, simmer, covered, 10 minutes. Add potatoes and parsnip, simmer, covered, until just tender.

4 Add broccoli, cauliflower, mushrooms and water, simmer, covered, about 5 minutes or until all the vegetables are tender.

5 Pappadams: Heat oil in a small skillet, add pappadams, 1 or 2 at a time. Cook on 1 side for a few seconds until puffed and golden.

6 Turn pappadams with tongs and cook other side; drain on absorbent paper.

TOMATO, MINT AND LIME SALAD

Important Points

- Tomatoes are available all year round, but are at their best in late summer.
- Choose well-shaped, uniformly red, firm tomatoes, heavy for their size and free from damaged skin.
- Tomatoes can quickly become over-ripe in hot weather. Before that happens, it's best to place them in the vegetable crisper of the refrigerator.
- Chili powder is very hot; adjust amount according to your own taste.
- Substitute lemon juice for lime juice, if desired.
- Recipe can be made 1 hour ahead and stored, covered, in the refrigerator.
- Not suitable to freeze.

You Need

2 medium (about ½lb) tomatoes
3 green onions
¼ cup chopped fresh mint
3 tablespoons fresh lime juice
1 teaspoon sugar
⅛ teaspoon chili powder

1 Remove tomato cores with a sharp knife. Cut tomatoes into wedges lengthways. Chop onions. Combine tomatoes, onions and mint in a medium bowl.

2 Using a small wire whisk, mix together juice, sugar and chili in a small jug, pour over tomato mixture; stir gently.

YOGURT WITH CUCUMBER

Important Points

● Choose a firm, bright green cucumber; avoid those with damaged skin.

● Wash cucumber, dry well and store in the vegetable crisper in the refrigerator.

● Chopped cucumber is sprinkled with coarse (kosher) salt to extract excess moisture; this is known as degorging.

● Leave out the cuminseed and add some chopped fresh mint or cilantro for variety, if you like.

● Recipe can be made a day ahead and stored, covered, in the refrigerator.

● Not suitable to freeze.

You Need

1 small (about 6oz) green cucumber
1 teaspoon coarse (kosher) salt
1 teaspoon cuminseed
2 green onions
¾ cup plain yogurt
2 teaspoons fresh lemon juice

1 Peel cucumber with a vegetable peeler. Cut in half lengthways, scoop out seeds with a teaspoon; discard seeds. Chop cucumber finely.

2 Place cucumber in a strainer, sprinkle with salt. Place strainer over a bowl, stand 15 minutes. Rinse cucumber under cold water; drain well.

3 Place cuminseed in a small saucepan, stir over low heat until lightly browned and fragrant.

4 Chop onions finely. Combine onions, cucumber, cuminseed, yogurt and lemon juice in a bowl; mix well.

NUTTY RICE

Important Points

- There are many types of rice available and many ways of cooking it. We used long-grain rice.
- In this recipe, we have steamed the rice; this is known as the absorption method.
- Use a heavy-based pan with a tight-fitting lid. Do not remove lid during the steaming process.
- Not suitable to freeze.
- Suitable to microwave.

You Need

1 cup (7oz) rice
1 tablespoon ghee
1 clove garlic, minced
1 teaspoon coriander seeds
6 cardamom pods
1 cinnamon stick
1½ cups boiling water
3 tablespoons golden raisins
3 tablespoons roasted unsalted cashews

1 Place rice in a strainer, rinse under cold water until water runs clear; drain well.

2 Heat ghee in a medium saucepan, add garlic, coriander seeds, cardamom pods and cinnamon stick, cook, stirring, over low heat for 2 minutes.

3 Add rice to the saucepan on the stove, stir until rice is coated with ghee and spices. Add boiling water, stir rice with a spoon. Cover the saucepan with a tight-fitting lid, reduce heat to the lowest heat, steam for about 15 minutes or until water is absorbed and rice is tender.

4 Remove the saucepan from the heat, remove the lid, discard the cinnamon stick, stir rice with a fork, stand 2 minutes. Stir in raisins and cashews.

■ PORK SCHNITZELS WITH TOMATO SAUCE
■ BUTTERED SPINACH

A schnitzel is a very thin cutlet which is coated with bread crumbs, then lightly fried; there are many varieties of schnitzel. We like to use both packaged and fresh bread crumbs because the combination both clings and cooks better. Serves 4.

SHOPPING LIST

4 small (about 15oz) pork leg cutlets
14½oz can whole peeled tomatoes
2 bunches (about 2¾lb) spinach
1 egg
milk
all-purpose flour
packaged unseasoned bread crumbs
fresh bread crumbs
light olive oil
butter
dried mixed herbs
sugar
chicken instant bouillon
ground nutmeg

WORK PLAN

1 Prepare pork, cover with crumbs, refrigerate.

2 Cook tomato sauce.

3 Trim and wash spinach.

4 Put pork on to cook.

5 Cook spinach.

6 Turn pork over.

7 Drain spinach, toss with butter.

8 Serve pork schnitzels with tomato sauce and buttered spinach.

PORK SCHNITZELS WITH TOMATO SAUCE

Important Points

● Pork has become leaner. Pork should be pale pink, smooth and finely grained; any fat should be white and firm.

● Keep pork in the meat keeper or in the coldest part of the refrigerator on a plate or on a rack over a plate, lightly covered with baking paper, then plastic wrap or foil, allowing the air to circulate around meat.

● It is important not to overcook pork or it will be dry and tough.

● Veal steaks and lamb chops are also suitable cuts of meat to crumb and fry.

● Use packaged unseasoned and fresh bread crumbs in equal proportions; this gives a good-colored but slightly soft coating on the pork. See Techniques section at the back of this book for how to prepare bread crumbs.

● A combination of oil and butter is used for frying. The butter is for flavor, the oil keeps the butter from burning.

● Fry in an uncovered, wide skillet, a little at a time. Adding too much food at a time lowers the temperature of the oil mixture and interferes with the browning.

● Pork schnitzels can be crumbed a day ahead and stored, covered, in the refrigerator.

● Serve pork schnitzels immediately with tomato sauce and buttered spinach.

● Serve with baked jacket potatoes, if desired; see page 108.

● Tomato sauce can be made 2 days ahead and stored, covered, in the refrigerator.

● Schnitzels and sauce not suitable to freeze.

● Schnitzels not suitable to microwave. Tomato sauce suitable to microwave.

You Need

4 small (about 15oz) pork leg cutlets
1 egg
¼ cup milk
¼ cup all-purpose flour
½ cup packaged unseasoned bread crumbs
½ cup fresh bread crumbs
3 tablespoons light olive oil
2 tablespoons (¼ stick) butter

Tomato Sauce
14½oz can whole peeled tomatoes
½ teaspoon dried mixed herbs
½ teaspoon sugar
½ teaspoon chicken instant bouillon

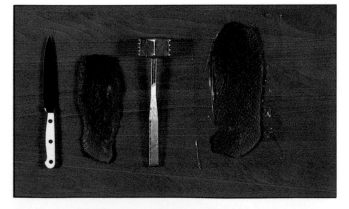

1 Using a sharp knife, cut any membrane from around edge of pork to prevent pork curling up during cooking. Place pork between 2 sheets of plastic wrap or baking paper and gently beat with a meat mallet or a rolling pin until fairly thin. Trim pork into neat shape; cut large pieces in half for easier cooking.

2 Whisk egg and milk together in a medium bowl. Dust pork lightly with flour, shake away excess flour. Dip pork into egg mixture. Coat with combined bread crumbs, press crumbs on firmly. Refrigerate, covered, 1 hour before cooking.

3 Add oil and butter to a large skillet, heat until butter is foamy. Add schnitzels 1 or 2 at a time, cook over medium heat for about 3 minutes on each side or until crumbs are golden brown and pork is just cooked. Drain on absorbent paper. Serve with tomato sauce.

4 Tomato Sauce: Place undrained tomatoes in medium saucepan, crush with fork. Add remaining ingredients, bring to boil, reduce heat, simmer, uncovered, for about 5 minutes or until slightly thickened, stirring occasionally. Blend or process until smooth, if desired.

BUTTERED SPINACH

Important Points

● Spinach is available all year round. Choose fresh, bright green leaves.
● Store spinach in the vegetable crisper or in a plastic bag in the refrigerator and use as soon as possible.
● Spinach can be cooked and drained several hours ahead; store, covered, in the refrigerator. Reheat in the pan with butter and serve immediately.
● To drain spinach well, squeeze between 2 plates or squeeze in the hand.
● Not suitable to freeze.
● Suitable to microwave.

You Need

2 bunches (about 2¾lb) spinach
2 tablespoons (¼ stick) butter
⅛ teaspoon ground nutmeg

1 Remove stems from spinach. Wash spinach thoroughly and place the wet leaves into a large saucepan. Do not add extra water.

2 Cover the saucepan, cook over medium heat about 3 minutes, shaking pan occasionally, or until spinach is limp. Drain spinach, rinse under cold water; drain. Heat butter in pan, add spinach and nutmeg, stir until hot.

■ HAM AND CORN FRITTATA
■ BEET AND RED CABBAGE SALAD
■ SPINACH SALAD WITH AVOCADO

A frittata is a substantial, Italian-style omelet that is served flat, not folded like a French omelet. It's a great way to make a meal out of leftovers such as chopped meat, poultry, fish and vegetables of your choice. We have served ours with 2 pretty salads, each with a different dressing. Serves 4.

SHOPPING LIST

2 medium (about 10oz) potatoes
2 medium (about 10oz) onions
1 medium (about ¼lb) tomato
½ small avocado
1 bunch (about 1¼lb) spinach
2½oz sugar snap peas
1 medium (about ¼lb) beet
¼ medium (about ¾lb) red cabbage
1 medium (about 6oz) orange
fresh parsley
7oz cooked ham
4oz can creamed corn
4 eggs
Parmesan cheese
butter
salad oil
milk
cider vinegar
poppy seeds
walnuts
bottled herb and garlic dressing

WORK PLAN

1 Prepare beet and red cabbage salad, cover, refrigerate.

2 Chop onions for frittata, cook onions.

3 Prepare remaining ingredients for frittata.

4 Slice tomato, wash and dry spinach.

5 Put frittata on to cook.

6 Make avocado dressing.

7 Prepare spinach salad, drizzle with dressing.

8 Serve ham and corn frittata with beet and red cabbage salad, and spinach salad with avocado.

HAM AND CORN FRITTATA

Important Points

- A frittata is a good way of using up leftovers. Add chopped, cooked meat, poultry, fish and vegetables of your choice. You can use any kind of ham.
- A nonstick pan is a handy piece of equipment although not essential.
- Ham and corn frittata can be served hot or cold.
- Cold frittata can be cut into small pieces and served with drinks at a party.
- Not suitable to freeze.
- Not suitable to microwave.

You Need

2 medium (about 10oz) onions
3 tablespoons butter
2 medium (about 10oz) potatoes
7oz cooked ham
4 eggs

4oz can creamed corn
¼ cup chopped fresh parsley
1 tablespoon butter, extra
¼ cup grated Parmesan cheese

1 Chop onions finely. Heat butter in a small saucepan, add onions, cook, covered, over low heat about 20 minutes, or until onions are very soft but not colored; stir occasionally.

2 Wash and peel potatoes; grate coarsely. Chop ham.

3 Beat eggs lightly in a medium bowl with a wire whisk or fork; the yolks should be just mixed through the whites. Add onion mixture, potatoes, ham, corn and parsley; mix well with a fork.

4 Heat extra butter in a 10 inch diameter skillet, swirl to coat skillet evenly. Add egg mixture, spread evenly over base of skillet. Cook over low heat, without stirring, for about 10 minutes or until set and well browned underneath. Sprinkle cheese over frittata, cook frittata under hot broiler until top is set and well browned.

38

BEET AND RED CABBAGE SALAD

Important Point

● Salad can be made 3 hours ahead and stored, covered, in the refrigerator.

You Need

2½oz sugar snap peas
1 medium (about ¼lb) beet
¼ medium (about ¾lb) red cabbage
1 teaspoon grated orange zest

3 tablespoons fresh orange juice
¼ cup salad oil
4 teaspoons cider vinegar
1 teaspoon poppy seeds

1 Trim tops and strings from peas. Peel and grate beet, shred cabbage. Combine vegetables in bowl.

2 Whisk remaining ingredients together in a small bowl, add to cabbage mixture; mix well.

SPINACH SALAD WITH AVOCADO

Important Point

● Salad can be made an hour ahead and stored, covered, in refrigerator.

You Need

1 medium (about ¼lb) tomato
1 bunch (about 1¼lb) spinach
¾ cup walnuts

½ small avocado
¼ cup bottled herb and garlic dressing
¼ cup milk

1 Cut tomato into thin wedges. Wash spinach leaves, drain; tear spinach into pieces. Combine tomato, spinach and walnuts in a large bowl, toss lightly.

2 Peel and chop avocado. Mash avocado with a fork in a medium bowl, whisk in dressing and milk (or blend or process until smooth), drizzle over spinach salad.

■ CORNED BEEF WITH CREAMY ONION SAUCE

■ TOMATO LENTILS

You need to bring this cut of beef up to the boil, drain away the water, then boil again until the meat is tender; the first boiling extracts excess salt gained during the corning (curing) process. Serves 4.

SHOPPING LIST

2lb piece fresh corned beef
2 small (about 5oz) onions
1 medium (about 5oz) onion
2 small (about 5oz) carrots
1 medium (about ¼lb) tomato
fresh parsley
fresh tarragon
garlic
black peppercorns
dark brown sugar
brown vinegar
butter
olive oil
milk
all-purpose flour
7oz brown lentils
chicken broth
ground cumin

WORK PLAN

1 Prepare vegetables for corned beef.

2 Cover beef with water, bring to the boil; drain.

3 Cover beef with water again, add remaining ingredients, cover, cook for 1 hour.

4 Prepare vegetables for creamy onion sauce and tomato lentils.

5 Put lentils on to cook.

6 Make creamy onion sauce.

7 Stand corned beef for 5 minutes before serving with creamy onion sauce and tomato lentils.

CORNED BEEF WITH CREAMY ONION SAUCE

Important Points

- The brisket and beef round are the two most popular cuts for corning. Corning is curing with a pickle solution of water, salt, sugar and spices. The brisket is cut from the breast; the round is cut from the thigh.

- Allow 25 to 30 minutes per 1lb for cooking time.

- If serving corned beef cold, allow it to cool in the cooking liquid; this keeps it moist.

- Corned beef is traditionally served with boiled or steamed cabbage and carrots. As an alternative, we have served it with tomato lentils.

- For tips on making a smooth white sauce, see Important Points for mushroom lasagne, and cauliflower and broccoli au gratin; see pages 46 and 86.

- Recipe is best made close to serving. Beef can be cooked a day ahead and served cold; store in refrigerator.

- Not suitable to freeze.

- Beef not suitable to microwave. Sauce suitable to microwave.

You Need

2lb piece fresh corned beef
1 small (about 2½oz) onion
1 small (about 2½oz) carrot

8 black peppercorns
1 teaspoon dark brown sugar
2 teaspoons brown vinegar

1 Place beef in a large saucepan, cover with cold water, bring to the boil. Lift beef from the saucepan with 2 large slotted metal spoons; drain in a colander; discard water. This process removes excess salt.

2 Cut onion in half; see Techniques section. Peel and chop carrot.

3 Return beef to the large saucepan, cover with cold water, add onion halves, carrot, peppercorns, sugar and vinegar. Bring to the boil, simmer, covered, for 1 hour. Skim surface of water occasionally with a metal spoon to remove any froth, etc., that may appear.

4 Remove beef from the saucepan, drain. Discard liquid, vegetables and peppercorns unless you plan to cool beef in the liquid to serve it cold. Stand beef, covered with foil, for 5 minutes before slicing. Serve with creamy onion sauce.

CREAMY ONION SAUCE

You Need

1 medium (about 5oz) onion
2 tablespoons (¼ stick) butter
4 teaspoons all-purpose flour

1 cup milk
4 teaspoons chopped fresh parsley

1 Chop onion finely. Heat butter in a small saucepan, add onion, cook, covered, over low heat for about 10 minutes or until very soft, stirring onion occasionally.

2 Add flour to pan, stir over heat until bubbly. Remove from heat, gradually stir in milk, return to heat, stir until sauce boils and thickens; stir in parsley.

TOMATO LENTILS

Important Points

● Recipe can be made a day ahead and stored, covered, in the refrigerator.
● Suitable to freeze.
● Suitable to microwave.

You Need

1 small (about 2½oz) onion
1 small (about 2½oz) carrot
1 medium (about ¼lb) tomato
4 teaspoons olive oil
1 clove garlic, minced

1 cup (7oz) brown lentils
1½ cups chicken broth
½ teaspoon ground cumin
2 teaspoons chopped fresh tarragon

1 Chop onion finely. Peel and chop carrot finely. Peel tomato, remove seeds and chop tomato. Heat oil in a medium saucepan, add onion, garlic, and carrot, cook, stirring, over medium heat until onion is soft.

2 Wash lentils well; drain. Add lentils, broth and cumin to the saucepan, bring to the boil, stirring. Simmer, covered, for about 20 minutes or until lentils are tender. Stir in tomato and tarragon, stir until hot.

MUSHROOM LASAGNE
GREEN SALAD

There are countless versions of lasagne, depending on your choice of ingredients. It makes a popular meal in one dish, and usually consists of pasta sheets layered in a casserole dish with other ingredients. The filling can be vegetarian, such as our mushroom recipe, or you can substitute a hearty meat sauce. We have used no-boil lasagne noodles to simplify cooking. The versatile green salad can accompany many other dishes. Serves 4.

SHOPPING LIST

1½lb flat mushrooms
1 medium (about ¾lb) leek
1 medium Boston lettuce
1 small (about 6oz) green cucumber
½ small (about 2½oz) green bell pepper
3 green onions
2 stalks celery
1 large lemon
fresh chives
fresh basil
garlic
Parmesan cheese
6 no-boil lasagne noodles
fresh bread crumbs
pine nuts
butter
all-purpose flour
milk
1 egg
paprika
salad oil
dry mustard
sugar

WORK PLAN

1 Prepare cheese sauce.

2 Prepare mushroom filling.

3 Assemble lasagne and bake.

4 Prepare salad vegetables.

5 Prepare salad dressing, pour over salad vegetables and mix gently.

6 Serve mushroom lasagne with green salad.

MUSHROOM LASAGNE

Important Points

- Mushrooms are available all year round. Choose firm, dry, clean, undamaged mushrooms. Avoid withered ones.
- Store mushrooms in a brown paper or calico bag in the refrigerator for 5 to 7 days.
- Mushrooms do not need to be peeled or washed, just wiped with a damp cloth.
- Remove outer layer of leeks if dirty or damaged. Trim roots and coarse green tops from leeks and wash white leaves well before using; see Techniques section. Store leeks in the vegetable crisper in the refrigerator.
- When making the cheese sauce, stir the flour and butter in a saucepan over low heat until well combined and thick. This mixture is called a roux; see Terms section. Making the roux will take about 30 seconds to 1 minute, depending on the type of saucepan and the degree of heat. This will remove the raw taste of the flour in the sauce. Stirring too long over the heat, however, will brown the flour and will result in a brown sauce.
- Remove the saucepan from the heat before adding the milk to prevent a lumpy sauce.
- Give the sauce a good hard boil, stirring constantly, after it thickens to give it a good shine.
- If preferred, make lasagne with a meat sauce, using the bolognese sauce recipe from spaghetti bolognese (see page 68) instead of the mushroom filling.
- No-boil lasagne noodles require no pre-cooking.
- Lasagne can be made a day ahead and stored, covered, in the refrigerator.
- For bread crumbs, see page 118..
- Mushroom Lasagne not suitable to freeze. Cheese sauce and mushroom filling suitable to microwave.

You Need

¼ cup (½ stick) butter
½ cup all-purpose flour
2½ cups milk
¼ cup grated Parmesan cheese
1 egg, lightly beaten
3 tablespoons chopped fresh basil
6 no-boil lasagne noodles
3 tablespoons fresh bread crumbs
4 teaspoons grated Parmesan cheese, extra
3 tablespoons pine nuts
¼ teaspoon paprika

Mushroom Filling

1½lb flat mushrooms
1 medium (about ¾lb) leek
2 tablespoons (¼ stick) butter
2 cloves garlic, minced
1 teaspoon chopped fresh chives

1 Melt butter in a medium saucepan, add flour, stir constantly over low heat until well combined and thick. Remove the saucepan from heat, gradually stir in milk. Return the saucepan to heat and stir until sauce boils and thickens. Stand mixture for a few minutes; stir in cheese, egg and basil.

2 Lightly grease an ovenproof dish (6 cup capacity). Spread one-third of the mushroom filling over the base of the prepared dish. Cover with 3 lasagne noodles, half the remaining mushroom filling, half the cheese sauce, then remaining lasagne noodles.

3 Top with remaining mushroom filling and cheese sauce. Sprinkle with combined bread crumbs, extra cheese, pine nuts and paprika. Place lasagne on a baking sheet, bake, uncovered, in 350°F oven for about 45 minutes or until browned and lasagne is hot.

4 Mushroom Filling: Slice mushrooms thinly. Slice white part of leek lengthways, wash and chop finely. Heat butter in a large saucepan, add mushrooms, leek and garlic, cook, stirring, until mushrooms are soft and liquid evaporated; stir in chives; drain.

GREEN SALAD

Important Points

- Choose firm, fresh lettuce; store in vegetable crisper of the refrigerator for up to 5 days, wrapped in damp tea-towel.
- Use any combination of lettuce. After washing, drain and shake or spin-dry (a salad spinner is useful).
- Salad can be mixed with the hands to ensure even distribution of dressing.
- Basic French dressing can be made in larger quantities and stored, covered, in the refrigerator for a week. Small quantities can then be flavored as required, for example, with minced garlic or chopped fresh herbs.
- Salad vegetables can be prepared about 3 hours ahead and stored, covered, in the refrigerator.
- Not suitable to freeze.

You Need

1 medium Boston lettuce
1 small (about 6oz) green cucumber
½ small (about 2½oz) green bell pepper
3 green onions
2 stalks celery, chopped

Basic French Dressing

⅓ cup salad oil
3 tablespoons lemon juice or white vinegar
¼ teaspoon dry mustard
¼ teaspoon sugar

1 Remove any coarse and damaged outer leaves of lettuce. Break lettuce into small pieces, wash and drain well. Trim away about ½ inch from each end of cucumber, slice cucumber thinly. Remove stem, seeds and membrane from pepper (seeds are hot), slice pepper thinly; chop onions. Combine all ingredients in bowl.

2 Basic French Dressing: Combine oil, juice, mustard and sugar in a bowl or jug; whisk with wire whisk (or combine all ingredients in a screw-top jar; shake well). Add dressing to lettuce mixture; mix gently.

■ BROILED LAMB CHOPS WITH ANCHOVY BUTTER
■ MASHED POTATOES
■ RATATOUILLE

For terrific results when broiling chops, you should preheat the broiler to the highest setting and cook them quickly on both sides to seal in the juices and all the taste. Good quality chops will be the most tender. We have enhanced the delicate lamb flavor with piquant anchovy butter, and served the chops with fluffy mashed potatoes and ratatouille, a colorful vegetable dish of French origin. Serves 4.

SHOPPING LIST

6 to 8 lamb sirloin chops
4 medium (about 1¼lb) old potatoes
1 medium (about 5oz) onion
1 medium (about 10oz) eggplant
2 medium (about 7oz) zucchini
8 small (about 3½oz) yellow pattypan squash
1 small (about 5oz) red bell pepper
1 small (about 5oz) green bell pepper
1 lemon
garlic
fresh parsley
fresh thyme
fresh basil
14½oz can whole peeled tomatoes
2oz can flat fillets of anchovies
coarse (kosher) salt
butter
milk
olive oil

WORK PLAN

1 Make anchovy butter and refrigerate.

2 Chop eggplant and leave to degorge; see Important Points.

3 Prepare remaining vegetables and herbs for ratatouille.

4 Prepare potatoes.

5 Rinse eggplant and begin to cook ratatouille.

6 Put potatoes on to cook.

7 Put chops on to broil.

8 Finish ratatouille.

9 Turn chops.

10 Remove anchovy butter from the refrigerator and slice.

11 Mash potatoes.

12 Serve broiled lamb chops with anchovy butter, mashed potatoes and ratatouille.

BROILED LAMB CHOPS

Important Points

- Lamb is at its best during spring. Store lamb in the meat keeper or in the coldest part of the refrigerator on a plate or a rack over a plate, loosely covered with baking paper, then plastic wrap or foil, allowing air to circulate around the lamb.
- Use tender cuts of lamb for broiling and frying; for example, sirloin, rib and loin chops.
- Trim away fat before cooking, if desired. Bring meat to room temperature before cooking, if possible.
- Preheat broiler on highest setting. The outside of the meat must be seared, that is, cooked quickly to seal the surface and retain juices.
- Do not overcook lamb or it will be dry and tough. Time will depend on the cut used and the thickness of the cut.
- If the cut is thick and you are finding it hard to cook the meat through, either move the broiler tray down a position away from the heat, or reduce the heat of the broiler after browning both sides.
- Use tongs to turn lamb; a fork will pierce the meat and allow juices to escape.
- Serve broiled lamb chops immediately.
- Not suitable to freeze.
- Not suitable to microwave.

You Need

6 to 8 lamb sirloin chops

1 Preheat broiler on highest setting, place chops slightly apart on the broiler tray.

2 Broil chops on 1 side for about 3 minutes or until browned. Turn chops with tongs, broil for about 3 more minutes, until browned, then broil until cooked as desired, turning once more.

ANCHOVY BUTTER

Important Points

- Leave butter to soften at room temperature before combining with other ingredients.
- Rinse anchovy fillets under water to reduce saltiness; pat dry with absorbent paper.
- You can serve anchovy butter with broiled fish or broiled chicken, if desired.
- Anchovy butter suitable to freeze.

You Need

3 anchovy fillets
3oz (¾ stick) butter
½ teaspoon fresh lemon juice
4 teaspoons chopped fresh parsley

1 Rinse anchovies under cold water, pat dry with absorbent paper. Chop anchovies finely. Place anchovies, butter, juice and parsley in a medium bowl, mash with a fork until well combined.

2 Transfer mixture onto a piece of foil, roll foil around mixture, shaping into a log; refrigerate until firm.

MASHED POTATOES

Important Points

- Choose firm, well-shaped potatoes, free from blemishes, cuts and sprouts. Avoid green potatoes. Store in a cool, dark, dry place with good ventilation.
- It is best to use "old" potatoes for mashed potatoes; ask your local market or supermarket.
- Cut potatoes into even-sized pieces for uniformity of cooking. Do not overcook potatoes; they will be watery.
- Never use a blender or a food processor to mash potatoes or they will become gluey.
- The consistency of mashed potatoes can vary from a firm to a more creamy texture, depending on your taste.
- Finely chopped onion and chopped fresh parsley can be stirred into mashed potatoes before serving, if desired. To chop onions and parsley, see Techniques section.
- Serve mashed potatoes immediately.
- Not suitable to freeze.
- Suitable to microwave.

You Need

4 medium (about 1¼lb) old potatoes
1 tablespoon butter
¼ cup milk, approximately

1 Peel potatoes and cut each into 4 even-sized pieces. Place potatoes in a medium saucepan, add enough cold water to just cover potatoes.

2 Cook, covered, on high heat until potatoes boil. Reduce heat to a gentle boil. Cook, covered, for about 15 minutes or until potatoes are soft; test for tenderness with a skewer or fork.

3 Drain potatoes in a strainer, return potatoes to the saucepan and mash with a potato masher or fork, or push the potatoes through a strainer.

4 Add butter and half the milk to potatoes in the saucepan, beat with a wooden spoon until butter is melted. Return the saucepan to low heat, beat in enough of the remaining milk to give desired consistency.

RATATOUILLE

Important Points

● Eggplants are available all year round. Choose firm eggplants with a smooth skin, heavy for their size, and free from dark brown spots.

● Store eggplants in the vegetable crisper of the refrigerator.

● Eggplants are sprinkled with salt to remove excess moisture and any bitterness; this is called degorging. This process also helps to prevent eggplants from absorbing excess oil during cooking.

● Vegetables for ratatouille are best fried separately as they cook at different rates.

● Ratatouille can be served on its own as a starter with fresh crusty bread or served hot as a sauce for pasta, or as an accompaniment to meat.

● To chop herbs, see Techniques section.

● Ratatouille can be made a day ahead and stored, covered, in the refrigerator. Serve hot or cold. To reheat ratatouille, place in a medium saucepan and stir gently over medium heat until heated through.

● Not suitable to freeze.

● Not suitable to microwave.

You Need

1 medium (about 10oz) eggplant
2 teaspoons coarse (kosher) salt
14½oz can whole peeled tomatoes
2 medium (about 7oz) zucchini
1 small (about 5oz) red bell pepper
1 small (about 5oz) green bell pepper
8 small (about 3½oz) yellow pattypan squash
1 medium (about 5oz) onion
¼ cup olive oil
4 teaspoons olive oil, extra
2 cloves garlic, minced
1 teaspoon chopped fresh thyme
4 teaspoons chopped fresh basil

1 Trim away eggplant stem. Cut eggplant into ½ inch cubes. Place in a strainer, sprinkle with salt, stand 30 minutes to degorge; see Terms section.

2 Place eggplant in a strainer, rinse eggplant under cold water to remove salt; pat dry with absorbent paper. Place undrained tomatoes in a medium bowl, crush with a fork or potato masher.

3 Trim away about ½ inch from each end of zucchini, cut zucchini into ½ inch slices. Cut peppers in half, remove stems, seeds and membranes. Chop peppers into 1¼ inch squares. Cut squash into quarters. Chop onion; see Techniques section.

4 Heat oil in a large skillet, fry zucchini, peppers, squash and eggplant separately until lightly browned. Lift each vegetable separately from skillet; drain on absorbent paper.

5 Heat extra oil in the skillet, add onion, cook, stirring, until onion is soft but not colored. Add garlic, thyme and crushed tomatoes. Bring to the boil, reduce heat, simmer, uncovered, until mixture is thick; stir mixture occasionally.

6 Stir eggplant, zucchini, peppers, squash and basil into tomato mixture. Stir over medium heat until well combined and heated through.

■ SALAD NICOISE

This famous salad is a delicious combination of foods common to the Nice region in France; it usually includes anchovies, tuna, hard-boiled eggs, tomatoes, lettuce, black olives, green beans and potatoes, but other ingredients can be added. Serves 4.

SHOPPING LIST

5oz green beans
5oz baby new potatoes
12 cherry tomatoes
lettuce
fresh chives
1 large lemon
2 x 7oz cans tuna
2oz can flat fillets of anchovies
black olives
capers
2 eggs
olive oil
white vinegar
1 loaf crusty bread (optional)

WORK PLAN

1 Cook eggs and cool, cut into quarters.

2 Cook potatoes and cool, cut in half.

3 Cook beans and refresh.

4 Prepare remaining ingredients for salad.

5 Prepare dressing.

6 Combine all ingredients, toss with dressing.

7 Serve salad nicoise with crusty bread, if desired.

SALAD NICOISE

Important Points

- This salad is a meal in itself; just serve with crusty bread. It also makes a good accompaniment; leave out the tuna and serve with fish or meat if you prefer.
- Stirring the eggs gently with a wooden spoon while the water comes to the boil will centralise the yolks. As a guide, after 3 minutes, the whites will be set but the yolks will be soft. After 5 minutes, the yolks will be set. After 8 to 10 minutes, the eggs will be hard-boiled.
- Choose young firm beans, free from blemishes, which snap easily. Store in the vegetable crisper or in a plastic bag in the refrigerator for up to 5 days.
- Do not overcook the beans; they should be still a little crisp and crunchy.
- Rinse beans quickly under cold water to refresh them; see Terms section. Refreshing sets the color and stops the cooking process.
- Potatoes are cooked in their jackets (ie, their skins), and served with their jackets on.
- Eggs, beans and potatoes can be cooked several hours in advance, cooled, covered, and stored in the refrigerator.
- Salad should be assembled just before serving.
- Recipe not suitable to freeze.
- Beans and potatoes suitable to microwave.

You Need

2 eggs
5oz green beans
5oz baby new potatoes
2oz can flat fillets of anchovies
⅓ cup (about 16) black olives
12 cherry tomatoes
6 lettuce leaves
2 x 7oz cans tuna

Dressing

1 teaspoon drained capers
¼ cup olive oil
2 tablespoons fresh lemon juice
1 teaspoon white vinegar
2 teaspoons chopped fresh chives

1 Place eggs in a medium saucepan, almost cover with cold water, stir eggs gently over high heat with a wooden spoon until the water comes to the boil. Boil, uncovered, for about 10 minutes.

2 Place eggs in the saucepan under cold water for about 1 minute or until eggs are cool enough to handle. Crack shells gently and leave in cold water for 5 minutes. This will stop a dark ring forming around the yolks. Peel away shells, starting from the broad end. Rinse eggs, pat dry with absorbent paper. Cut eggs in half and then cut each half into 2 wedges.

3 Cut or snap off each end of beans and remove any strings. Cut beans into 1½ inch lengths. Half fill a medium saucepan with water, bring water to the boil, add beans, allow water to return to the boil. Reduce heat, simmer gently, uncovered, about 1 minute or until beans are still a little crisp and crunchy.

4 To refresh beans, drain them in a strainer, rinse quickly under cold water, shake away excess water; pat beans dry with absorbent paper.

5 Place potatoes in a medium saucepan, barely cover with cold water, bring water to the boil. Reduce heat, simmer, uncovered, about 8 minutes or until potatoes feel soft when tested with a fork. Drain potatoes in a strainer; cool. Cut potatoes in half.

6 Drain anchovies in a small strainer, rinse gently under cold water; pat dry with absorbent paper. Cut olives in half and remove stones. Cut tomatoes in half. Tear lettuce leaves into pieces. Drain tuna in a strainer, break into large pieces.

7 Place eggs, beans, potatoes, anchovies, olives, tomatoes, lettuce and tuna in a large bowl, add dressing, toss lightly using 2 large spoons. Serve salad with fresh, crusty bread, if desired.

8 Dressing: Chop capers finely. Combine capers, oil, lemon juice, vinegar and chives in a medium bowl; whisk well using a wire whisk (or combine all ingredients in a screw-top jar; shake well).

MARINATED PORK

Important Points

● When marinating you need to start preparations earlier on the day or a day ahead.

● Marinating imparts added flavor to foods. It also helps to tenderize some cuts of meat.

● Store pork in the meat keeper or in the coldest part of the refrigerator on a plate or a rack over a plate, loosely covered with baking paper, then plastic wrap or foil, allowing air to circulate around the meat.

● Pork belly is usually fatty; trim, if desired. Pork country-style ribs are less fatty and require little trimming.

● You will need 2 to 3 pork pieces per person.

● Pork can be placed in the marinade and stored, covered, in the refrigerator for 3 hours or overnight.

● Serve marinated pork and fried rice with green salad, if desired; see page 47.

● Uncooked marinated pork is suitable to freeze.

● Not suitable to microwave.

You Need

8 slices pork belly or 8 country-style pork ribs

Marinade

½ cup light soy sauce
⅓ cup honey

½ teaspoon ground gingerroot
⅓ cup fresh orange juice
1 clove garlic, minced
4 teaspoons chopped fresh chives

1 Marinade: Combine sauce, honey, gingerroot, juice, garlic and chives in a small saucepan. Stir over low heat until honey is just melted and ingredients are well combined; cool marinade.

2 Pour marinade mixture over pork in shallow glass dish or bowl, cover, refrigerate for 3 hours or overnight. Turn pork occasionally with tongs.

3 Drain pork from marinade, reserve marinade. Cover the base of a roasting pan with foil (this will make washing-up easier). Place a wire rack in the pan, place pork on the rack.

4 Bake pork, uncovered, in 375°F oven, brushing occasionally (basting) with reserved marinade for about 50 minutes or until pork is well browned and cooked through.

FRIED RICE

Important Points

- A wok is ideal for cooking fried rice, but a large skillet will also do the job well.

- There are several methods for making fried rice. This is the easiest because it uses already-cooked rice; follow details for boiling rice in herbed rice (see page 99) but omit the herbs and butter. You will need ⅔ cup (4½oz) of uncooked rice to make 2 cups of cooked rice. We prefer to use long-grain rice.

- Fried rice can be used as an accompaniment as we have done here or can be made into a main meal by adding a variety of other ingredients; for example, small pieces of cooked meat, poultry or seafood. We have included omelet pieces for flavor and texture.

- Fried rice is best made just before serving.

- Not suitable to freeze.

- Not suitable to microwave.

You Need

1 small (about 5oz) red bell pepper
2oz button mushrooms
1 small (about 2½oz) carrot
1 stalk celery
2 eggs

4 teaspoons light olive oil
1 clove garlic, minced
½ teaspoon grated fresh gingerroot
2 teaspoons light soy sauce
2 cups cooked rice

1 Cut pepper in half lengthways, remove stem, seeds and membrane, chop pepper finely. Wipe mushrooms with a damp cloth, slice thinly. Peel carrot, chop finely. Cut celery crossways into thin slices.

2 Whisk eggs in small bowl. Heat oil in wok, transfer oil to small heatproof jug; reserve oil. Pour eggs into wok, tilt wok so eggs cover base, cook over medium heat until set. Transfer omelet to plate; cool.

3 Return reserved oil to the wok, add pepper, mushrooms, carrot, celery, garlic and gingerroot. Stir-fry constantly over high heat for about 1 minute or until vegetables are almost tender.

4 Add chopped omelet, soy sauce and rice. Stir-fry constantly over high heat for about 2 minutes or until mixture is heated through.

■ STEAK DIANE
■ POTATO AND ONION CASSEROLE
■ STEAMED BEANS AND CARROTS

For this famous dish, the tender steaks are quickly pan-fried and served with a simple, tasty cream sauce. The beans and carrots are easy, too, cooked in a steamer basket, but the potato and onion casserole takes much longer to cook so allow plenty of time for it. Serves 4.

SHOPPING LIST

4 (about 1¼lb) beef rib eye steaks
4 medium (about 1¼lb) old potatoes
1 medium (about 5oz) onion
¾lb green beans
4 medium (about 1lb) carrots
garlic
light olive oil
butter
1¼ cups heavy cream
brandy
Worcestershire sauce
chicken broth

WORK PLAN

1 Prepare and cook potato and onion casserole.

2 Prepare beans and carrots.

3 Trim steaks, put on to cook.

4 Put beans and carrots on to cook.

5 Make sauce for steaks.

6 Serve steak diane with potato and onion casserole and steamed beans and carrots.

STEAK DIANE

Important Points

- Store meat in the meat keeper or in the coldest part of the refrigerator on a plate or on a rack over a plate, loosely covered with baking paper, then plastic wrap or foil.
- Use tender cuts of meat for frying and broiling; for example, tenderloin, rib eye and sirloin.
- Trim away as much fat as possible from the steaks before cooking.
- It is preferable to bring steaks to room temperature before cooking.
- Do not overcook the steaks or they will be dry and tough.
- Cooking time will depend on the cut used and the thickness of the meat. To test doneness, see Techniques section.
- Use tongs to turn steaks; a fork will pierce them and allow juices to escape.
- Serve steaks immediately; they do not reheat successfully, but become tough and dry.
- Not suitable to freeze.
- Not suitable to microwave.

You Need

4 teaspoons light olive oil
4 (about 1¼lb) beef rib eye steaks
2 tablespoons (¼ stick) butter
2 cloves garlic, minced

1¼ cups heavy cream
4 teaspoons Worcestershire sauce
4 teaspoons brandy

1 Heat oil in a large skillet, add steaks, cook over high heat for about 3 minutes, turn with tongs, cook for about 3 more minutes, then cook as desired.

2 Using tongs, transfer steaks from the skillet to a large shallow dish or a plate, cover with foil, keep warm.

3 Heat butter until foamy in the same skillet, add garlic, stir over heat for 30 seconds.

4 Add cream, Worcestershire sauce and brandy to the skillet, stir over heat until sauce becomes slightly thickened. Pour sauce over steaks; serve immediately.

POTATO AND ONION CASSEROLE

Important Points

- Potato and onion casserole can be made a day ahead and stored, covered, in the refrigerator.
- Not suitable to freeze.
- Suitable to microwave.

You Need

4 medium (about 1¼lb) old potatoes
1 medium (about 5oz) onion

1 tablespoon butter, melted
1 cup chicken broth

1 Peel potatoes and onion, slice thinly. Layer into greased ovenproof dish (5 cup capacity). Pour broth over vegetables, brush with butter.

2 Bake, uncovered, in 325°F oven about 1½ hours or until potatoes are soft and top is browned.

STEAMED BEANS AND CARROTS

Important Points

- Not suitable to freeze.
- Suitable to microwave.

You Need

¾lb green beans
4 medium (about 1lb) carrots

1 Trim beans, remove strings. Peel carrots, cut into sticks. Place vegetables in a steamer basket.

2 Add 1 inch of water to saucepan, place steamer in pan, cover, steam vegetables 5 minutes or until tender.

SPAGHETTI BOLOGNESE

Important Points

- Ask your butcher for the best and leanest ground beef.

- Beef should be finely ground for best results.

- Store beef in the meat keeper or in the coldest part of the refrigerator on a plate loosely covered with plastic wrap or foil, allowing air to circulate around the beef.

- Use a large saucepan to brown beef and seal in juices.

- Long, slow cooking of the meat sauce gives richness of flavor.

- Cook onions slowly and gently over low heat, without browning; this is known as sweating the onions. They will become soft and less acidic.

- Cook all forms of pasta in plenty of boiling water; add pasta gradually to the water so it does not go off the boil.

- Cooking time for pasta varies according to individual manufacturer and freshness of the product. Pasta should be tender but firm. (This stage of cooking is known as "al dente".)

- To reheat pasta, place pasta in a large heatproof bowl, add enough boiling water to cover pasta and stand 1 minute; drain well. Pasta also reheats well in the microwave oven.

- Bolognese sauce can be used to replace the mushroom filling in mushroom lasagne; see page 46.

- Chili con Carne: For a simple variation of the bolognese sauce, add red kidney beans, sambal oelek and chopped fresh parsley to thickened bolognese sauce (end of step 4); stir gently until heated through. Serve chili con carne with herbed rice, if desired; see page 99.

- Serve bolognese sauce with pasta, sprinkle with grated Parmesan cheese, if desired.

- Bolognese sauce can be made 2 days ahead. Cool, then store, covered, in the refrigerator.

- Bolognese sauce suitable to freeze.

- Pasta suitable to cook in the microwave oven. Cooking time is about the same as for conventional cooking.

You Need

1 medium (about 5oz) onion
14½oz can whole peeled tomatoes
4 teaspoons olive oil
1 clove garlic, minced
1lb ground beef
1 cup water
1 teaspoon beef instant bouillon
2 tablespoons tomato paste
1 teaspoon mixed dried herbs
½ teaspoon sugar
1lb dried spaghetti pasta

Variation : Chili con Carne

8oz can red kidney beans
1 teaspoon sambal oelek
4 teaspoons chopped fresh parsley

1 Chop onion finely. Place undrained tomatoes in a medium bowl, crush with a fork or potato masher.

2 Heat oil in a large saucepan, add onion and garlic, cook, covered, over low heat for about 10 minutes or until onion is soft but not brown; stir mixture occasionally.

3 Add all the beef, cook, stirring, over high heat until beef is well browned and crumbly. Stir in the undrained crushed tomatoes.

4 Add water, instant bouillon, paste, herbs and sugar to pan. Bring mixture to the boil, stirring, reduce heat, simmer, uncovered, stirring occasionally, for about 1 hour or until sauce is thickened. Serve sauce with pasta.

5 Bring a large saucepan of water to the boil, gradually add pasta, boil, uncovered, until pasta is just tender. Use a pasta fork or tongs to lift pasta into a strainer; drain well.

Variation: Chili con Carne: Drain beans in a strainer, rinse under cold water; drain well. Add beans, sambal oelek and parsley to bolognese sauce, stir gently over medium heat until heated through.

■ BRAISED VEAL WITH MUSHROOM SAUCE
■ POLENTA TRIANGLES
■ BROILED BELL PEPPERS

Braising is a method of slowly cooking meat in a pan with a tight-fitting lid, with a selection of chopped vegetables and a small amount of liquid, either broth or wine. Chop vegetables finely to release maximum flavor. We've made polenta triangles to serve with braised veal, but if you do not want to deep-fry the polenta you can serve it after adding the cheese. Polenta and bell peppers can be prepared a day ahead. Serves 4.

SHOPPING LIST

2lb rolled veal roast
1 small (about 2½oz) onion
1 small (about 2½oz) carrot
1 stalk celery
10oz button mushrooms
1 medium (about 7oz) green bell pepper
1 medium (about 7oz) red bell pepper
fresh thyme
garlic
yellow cornmeal
olive oil
butter
1 egg
Parmesan cheese
dry white wine
chicken broth
French mustard
cornstarch
all-purpose flour
oil for deep-frying

WORK PLAN

1 Cook polenta, spread into pan; refrigerate.

2 Prepare vegetables to braise.

3 Put veal on to cook.

4 Broil and peel peppers.

5 Toss peppers in oil, keep warm over low heat.

6 Deep-fry polenta; keep warm, covered loosely, in a 300°F oven.

7 Stand veal and make mushroom sauce.

8 Serve braised veal sliced with mushroom sauce, polenta triangles and broiled bell peppers.

BRAISED VEAL WITH MUSHROOM SAUCE

Important Points

- Suitable cuts include shoulder, breast and leg. Veal should be pink and lean. Store in the meat keeper or in the coldest part of refrigerator on a plate or a rack over a plate, loosely covered with baking paper, then plastic wrap or foil.
- Recipe can be made a day ahead and stored, covered, in refrigerator.
- Not suitable to freeze.
- Not suitable to microwave.

You Need

1 small (about 2½oz) onion
1 small (about 2½oz) carrot
1 stalk celery
4 teaspoons olive oil
4 teaspoons olive oil, extra
2lb rolled veal roast
½ cup dry white wine

Mushroom Sauce
10oz button mushrooms
1 tablespoon butter
1 clove garlic, minced
½ cup chicken broth
½ teaspoon French mustard
4 teaspoons cornstarch
4 teaspoons water

1 Chop onion, carrot and celery finely. Heat oil in a large skillet, add onion, carrot and celery, cook, stirring, over medium heat until onion is soft. Transfer vegetables to a medium heavy-based saucepan.

2 Reheat remaining oil and extra oil in skillet, add veal, cook over high heat, turning with tongs, until well browned all over. Transfer veal to saucepan on top of vegetables; add wine.

3 Bring wine and vegetable mixture to the boil, reduce heat, simmer, covered tightly, for about 1 hour or until veal is tender, turning occasionally. Remove veal from the saucepan to a warmed heatproof dish, cover with foil and stand 10 minutes before slicing. Strain pan juices, reserve juices for use in mushroom sauce; discard vegetables. Serve veal with mushroom sauce.

4 Mushroom Sauce: Wipe mushrooms with a damp cloth, slice thinly. Heat butter and garlic in a medium saucepan, add mushrooms, cook, stirring, until soft. Stir in reserved pan juices, broth and mustard. Blend cornstarch and water together in a small bowl with a teaspoon, stir into mixture in saucepan, stir constantly over heat until mixture boils and thickens slightly.

POLENTA TRIANGLES

Important Points

- For deep-frying, see Techniques section.
- Not suitable to freeze or microwave.

You Need

2 cups chicken broth
½ cup (3½oz) yellow cornmeal
¼ cup grated Parmesan cheese

1 egg yolk
⅓ cup all-purpose flour
oil for deep-frying

1 Grease a 3 inch x 10½ inch baking pan. Boil broth in saucepan, stir in cornmeal, simmer until thick. Stir in cheese and yolk. Spread into pan; refrigerate.

2 Turn polenta out of pan, cut into triangles. Roll polenta in flour, shake away excess flour. Half fill a saucepan with oil; deep-fry polenta until browned; drain.

BROILED BELL PEPPERS

Important Points

Not suitable to freeze.
Not suitable to microwave.

You Need

1 medium (about 7oz) green bell pepper
1 medium (about 7oz) red bell pepper

3 tablespoons olive oil
2 teaspoons chopped fresh thyme

1 Preheat broiler. Cut peppers lengthways into quarters. Cut away stem, seeds and membranes. Broil peppers skin-side-up until skin blisters and blackens.

2 Scrape skin from peppers, rinse under cold water, pat dry. Cut peppers into ¾ inch strips. Heat oil in a medium saucepan, stir in peppers and thyme.

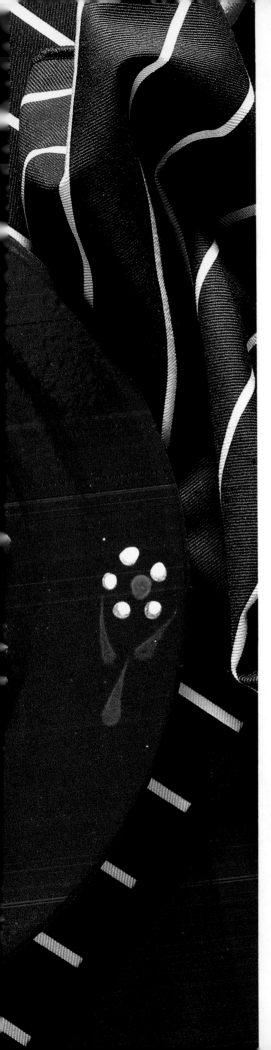

■ CHICKEN, BEAN AND TOMATO CASSEROLE

You can cut a chicken into pieces as we've done here or buy some chicken pieces, ready to transform into a hearty dinner with fresh tomatoes and canned garbanzo beans. Serves 4.

SHOPPING LIST

3lb chicken
6 medium (about 1½lb) tomatoes
2 medium (about 10oz) onions
1 small fresh red chili pepper
8¾oz can garbanzo beans
fresh basil
tomato paste
dry white wine
all-purpose flour
butter
olive oil
chicken broth
sugar
1 loaf crusty bread

WORK PLAN

1 Cut up chicken.

2 Peel and chop tomatoes.

3 Chop onion and chili pepper.

4 Put casserole on to cook.

5 Drain garbanzo beans.

6 Chop basil.

7 Add garbanzo beans and basil to casserole.

8 Serve chicken, bean and tomato casserole with fresh crusty bread.

CHICKEN, BEAN AND TOMATO CASSEROLE

Important Points

- The chicken we used is also suitable for roasting in the oven or cooking whole in a pot on top of the stove.
- Store fresh, uncooked chicken in the meat keeper or in the coldest part of the refrigerator on a plate or on a rack over a plate, loosely covered with baking paper, then plastic wrap or foil, allowing air to circulate around the chicken. Use chicken within 2 days of purchase.
- We show you how to cut a whole chicken into serving-sized pieces for this casserole. You can also buy chicken pieces; you will need 2lb chicken pieces for 4 servings.
- Chicken must be cooked all the way through. To test for doneness, pierce chicken with a skewer in the thickest part of the flesh or cut chicken; the juices should run clear.
- To peel tomatoes and chop onions, see Techniques section. For chicken broth, see Glossary.
- Chili peppers are available in many different types and sizes. Use tight rubber gloves when chopping fresh chili peppers as they can burn your skin.
- Dried garbanzo beans can be used instead of canned garbanzo beans. Use ½ cup (3½oz) dried garbanzo beans instead of an 8¾oz can of garbanzo beans. Place dried garbanzo beans in a large bowl, cover well with water, cover, stand overnight. Drain garbanzo beans, add to a large saucepan of water, bring to the boil, simmer, covered, for about 1 hour or until tender.
- Serve casserole with spinach salad, if desired; see page 39.
- Casserole can be made a day ahead, cooled, then stored, covered, in refrigerator.
- Suitable to freeze.
- Not suitable to microwave.

You Need

3lb chicken
6 medium (about 1½lb) tomatoes
2 medium (about 10oz) onions
1 small fresh red chili pepper
3 tablespoons all-purpose flour
¼ cup (½ stick) butter
4 teaspoons olive oil
¼ cup tomato paste
1½ cups chicken broth
½ cup dry white wine
1 teaspoon sugar
8¾oz can garbanzo beans
3 tablespoons shredded fresh basil

1 Place chicken breast-side-up on chopping board, and pull a leg away from the body. Cut through skin connecting leg to body, then find the joint between the leg and body and cut through this. Repeat on other side. The leg and thigh is called a maryland. Cut marylands into 2 pieces at joint to give thigh and leg (drumstick).

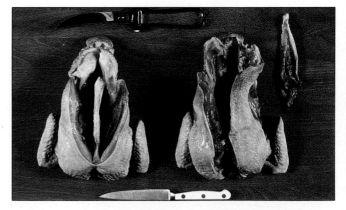

2 Carefully cut down each side of breast bone with a knife to free breast flesh a little. Use poultry shears or scissors to cut through the small bones close to the breast. Cut away the breast bone.

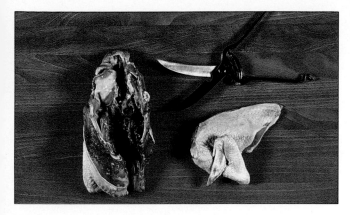

3 Open up chicken. Cut off each wing and breast with poultry shears, starting at the tail end and cutting up and through the wing bone near the neck.

4 Cut the breast into 2 pieces, leaving about one-third of the breast meat attached to the wing. The back portion of the carcass can be cut into 2 pieces and frozen for future use in soups or broth.

5 Peel tomatoes and chop roughly. Chop onions. Cut chili pepper in half (remember to use rubber gloves), remove stem and seeds, chop chili pepper finely.

6 Toss chicken in flour, shake away excess flour. Heat butter until foamy in a large skillet, add chicken pieces, a few pieces at a time, cook until well browned all over. Drain on absorbent paper.

7 Heat oil in the cleaned skillet, add onions, cook, stirring, over medium heat, until onions are soft. Stir in tomatoes, chili pepper, tomato paste, broth, wine and sugar. Bring to boil, simmer, uncovered, stirring occasionally, for about 10 minutes or until mixture is reduced by half. Return chicken to tomato mixture in skillet, cover skillet, simmer for about 20 minutes or until chicken is tender; stir mixture occasionally. To test chicken for doneness, pierce with a skewer in the thickest part of the flesh or cut chicken; juices should run clear.

8 Drain garbanzo beans in a strainer, rinse under cold water; drain well. Add garbanzo beans and basil to skillet, simmer, uncovered, until casserole is heated through, stirring occasionally.

■ CHICKEN AND PINEAPPLE STIR-FRY
■ CRISP NOODLES

A colorful and tempting stir-fry is one of the easiest meals to make. The secret of success is to use fresh ingredients and stir them constantly; chicken or any tender cut of meat are all good, and almost any vegetables are suitable. Add the firmest vegetables first, and the more tender ones a few minutes later. Serves 4.

SHOPPING LIST

1 medium (about 5oz) onion
1 medium (about 7oz) red bell pepper
½ bunch (about ¼lb) fresh asparagus
1 small (about 1¼lb) pineappple
fresh gingerroot
garlic
1¼lb chicken thighs, boned, skinned
oyster-flavored sauce
light soy sauce
chili sauce
light olive oil
cornstarch
rice vermicelli noodles
oil for deep-frying

WORK PLAN

1 Prepare vegetables, pineapple and chicken for stir-fry.

2 Stir-fry vegetables.

3 Cook noodles.

4 Stir-fry chicken, combine with vegetables and remaining ingredients.

5 Serve chicken and pineapple stir-fry immediately with crisp noodles.

CHICKEN AND PINEAPPLE STIR-FRY

Important Points

- Store uncooked chicken in the meat keeper or in the coldest part of the refrigerator on a plate or on a rack over a plate, loosely covered with plastic wrap or foil, allowing air to circulate around chicken. Use within 2 to 3 days.
- Use tender cuts of meat when stir-frying. Other suitable cuts are pork tenderloins, veal steak and beef tenderloin.
- Use a wok or very large skillet for best results.
- Keep stirring ingredients with the wok spoon in 1 hand, and shaking the wok or skillet with the other hand.
- Ingredients for the stir-fry can be prepared 3 hours ahead and stored, covered, in the refrigerator.
- Not suitable to freeze.
- Not suitable to microwave.

You Need

1 medium (about 5oz) onion
1 medium (about 7oz) red bell pepper
½ bunch (about ¼lb) fresh asparagus
1 small (about 1¼lb) pineapple
1¼lb chicken thighs, boned, skinned
4 teaspoons light olive oil
1 teaspoon grated fresh gingerroot

1 clove garlic, minced
4 teaspoons light olive oil, extra
4 teaspoons oyster-flavored sauce
4 teaspoons light soy sauce
1 teaspoon chili sauce
2 teaspoons cornstarch
3 tablespoons water

1 Cut onion in half and then slice. Cut pepper in half lengthways, remove stem, seeds and membrane. Cut pepper into thin slices. Snap off and discard tough ends of asparagus, cut diagonally into 1½ inch lengths.

2 Peel pineapple, remove "eyes" with the sharp point of a knife; cut pineapple in half lengthways. Remove and discard tough core; chop pineapple into pieces. Trim fat from chicken, cut chicken into ½ inch slices.

3 Heat oil in a wok or large skillet, add onion, gingerroot and garlic, stir-fry for 1 minute. Add pepper and asparagus, stir-fry for 1 minute. Remove vegetables from the wok to a plate while you cook the chicken.

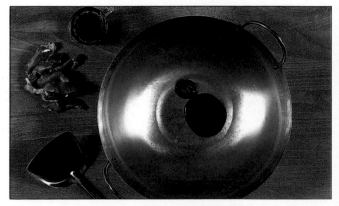

4 Heat extra oil in the wok, add oyster-flavored sauce, soy sauce and chili sauce, stir until combined. Add half of the chicken, stir-fry until tender, transfer from the wok to a plate. Cook remaining chicken the same way.

5 Return all vegetables, chicken and any juices to wok; add pineapple.

6 Blend cornstarch and water in a small jug with a teaspoon, add mixture to the wok, stir-fry until mixture boils and thickens.

CRISP NOODLES

Important Points

- Rice vermicelli noodles come in large, cellophane-wrapped bundles and can be stored indefinitely in a cool, dry cupboard.
- It is important to have the oil at the right temperature for deep-frying; to test heat of oil, see Techniques section.
- Noodles can be served hot or cold.
- Noodles can be cooked a day ahead and stored in an airtight container.
- Not suitable to freeze.
- Not suitable to microwave.

You Need

oil (about 6 cups) for deep-frying
3½oz rice vermicelli noodles

1 Heat oil until hot in a large heavy-based saucepan or wok, add about half the noodles, deep-fry until puffed and white (this will take about 5 seconds). Cook remaining noodles the same way.

2 Remove noodles from the saucepan with tongs; drain on absorbent paper. Serve noodles hot or cold.

ROASTED BEEF WITH GRAVY AND HORSERADISH CREAM
ROASTED POTATOES, PUMPKIN SQUASH AND ONIONS
CAULIFLOWER AND BROCCOLI AU GRATIN

When you're cooking a roasted dinner with all the trimmings, it's important to plan your timetable so that everything will be ready to serve at the same time. In our Important Points we tell you how to calculate roasting time for beef according to weight, then you can time the crispy potatoes, pumpkin squash and onions from that. You'll also need to make a basic white sauce for the "au gratin" dish. Our work plan helps you to organise the details in a fuss-free way. Serves 4.

SHOPPING LIST

2lb boned rolled sirloin of beef
4 medium (about 1¼lb) potatoes
14oz pumpkin squash
4 medium (about 1¼lb) onions
¼ small (about 10oz) cauliflower
7oz broccoli
fresh tarragon
garlic
seeded mustard
all-purpose flour
fresh bread crumbs
beef broth
dry red wine
Worcestershire sauce
bottled horseradish cream
French mustard
mayonnaise
sour cream
light olive oil
butter
beef dripping
milk
heavy cream
2oz cheddar cheese

WORK PLAN

1 Make the horseradish cream, cover, refrigerate.

2 Prepare potatoes, squash, onions, cauliflower and broccoli.

3 Boil or steam potatoes for 5 minutes. Prepare beef, put beef on to cook.

4 Cook cauliflower and broccoli.

5 Put potatoes, squash and onions in oven.

6 Make white sauce.

7 Put cauliflower and broccoli au gratin in oven.

8 Remove beef from oven, stand 10 minutes.

9 Make gravy.

10 Serve roasted beef with gravy, horseradish cream, roasted potatoes, pumpkin squash and onions, and cauliflower and broccoli au gratin.

ROASTED BEEF WITH GRAVY AND HORSERADISH CREAM

Important Points

- Beef should be stored in the meat keeper or in the coldest part of the refrigerator on a plate or a rack over a plate, loosely covered with baking paper, then plastic wrap or foil, allowing the air to circulate around the beef.

- Roasting means cooking in the oven with no liquid other than oil or fat. It is also known as baking. It is an economical means of cooking, as the vegetables can be cooked at the same time. Remember to preheat the oven.

- Weigh beef (or ask your butcher to weigh it), to establish cooking time; allow 40 to 60 minutes per 2lb for medium done beef and 30 to 40 minutes for rare beef – plus 10 minutes "standing time". The cooking time will vary with the thickness of the beef and the cut. Cuts suitable for roasting are: rib, sirloin, tenderloin, rump, chuck eye and round.

- Place beef on a wire rack in the roasting pan; this keeps the beef off the base of the roasting pan and prevents it from frying. This method also allows the heat to penetrate the beef more evenly.

- About every 20 to 30 minutes, baste the beef by spooning or brushing the juices in the roasting pan over it.

- For beef broth, see Glossary.

- When cooking time is up, stand beef on a serving plate in a warm place covered with foil. This standing period makes carving easier and gives an even color and juiciness throughout the beef.

- While the roast is standing, make the gravy in the roasting pan.

- Cooking a roast meal requires good organisation. One of the hardest parts is keeping everything hot while serving. It helps if the plates are hot; see Techniques section.

- Recipes are best made just before serving, although horseradish cream can be made 3 hours ahead and stored, covered, in the refrigerator.

- Not suitable to freeze.

- Not suitable to microwave.

You Need

1 tablespoon beef dripping or oil
2lb boned rolled sirloin of beef
4 teaspoons chopped fresh tarragon
4 teaspoons seeded mustard
2 cloves garlic, minced
2 tablespoons all-purpose flour
1½ cups beef broth
3 tablespoons dry red wine
1 tablespoon Worcestershire sauce

Horseradish Cream

2 tablespoons bottled horseradish cream
½ teaspoon French mustard
4 teaspoons mayonnaise
½ cup sour cream

1 Melt dripping or heat oil in a small saucepan. Place beef on a wire rack in a roasting pan, brush all over with dripping or oil. Bake, uncovered, in 350˚F oven for required cooking time; see Important Points. Baste every 20 to 30 minutes by spooning or brushing juices in pan over beef. Remove beef from oven.

2 Mix tarragon, mustard and garlic in a small bowl with a spoon. Spread mustard mixture over beef with a pallet knife or knife. Return beef to oven, bake about 10 minutes more or until beef is cooked as desired. Remove beef from the pan, cover with foil; remove string, stand. Serve sliced with gravy and horseradish cream.

3 To make gravy, pour away juices from the roasting pan, except for 3 tablespoons. Place the pan over high heat, add flour, stir constantly until flour is lightly browned, scrape as much of the colored bits and pieces from the base of the pan as you can. These will flavor and color the gravy. Remove the pan from heat.

4 Gradually stir in combined broth, wine and Worcestershire sauce. Return the pan to high heat, stir constantly until mixture boils and thickens; strain into a gravy boat or jug. (Or, strain gravy into a small saucepan, cover with lid to prevent a skin forming; reheat just before serving.)

5 Horseradish Cream: Place horseradish cream, mustard and mayonnaise into a medium bowl, stir with a wooden spoon until combined.

6 Place sour cream into a small bowl, whisk with a wire whisk until firm peaks form, fold into horseradish mixture with a spoon, cover, refrigerate until required.

ROASTED POTATOES, PUMPKIN SQUASH AND ONIONS

Important Points

- Choose firm potatoes free from blemishes, cuts and sprouts. Avoid green potatoes.
- Any type of pumpkin squash can be roasted or baked; these include the larger type or the smaller, sweeter varieties such as butternut or golden nugget.
- Brown onions are best for baking; try to choose onions of an even size, with thin skin. Avoid sprouting onions and those with excessively dry, crackling skin.
- It's best to roast vegetables in a shallow pan (such as a shallow baking pan); deep-sided pans tend to prevent the vegetables from browning. Vegetables can be roasted on the rack next to the beef; however, we prefer to roast the vegetables separately. Do not roast vegetables in the same pan as the meat as the juices can make the vegetables soggy.
- Recipe is best made just before serving.
- Not suitable to freeze.
- Not suitable to microwave except for preliminary cooking of the potatoes.

You Need

4 medium (about 1¼lb) potatoes
14oz pumpkin squash
4 medium (about 1¼lb) onions
4 teaspoons light olive oil

1 Prepare potatoes. Cut peeled potatoes in half, boil in water or steam for 5 minutes. Drain potatoes in a strainer, use tongs to place potatoes in a single layer on absorbent paper. Use fork to score upper rounded surface of potatoes; this will help potatoes crisp.

2 Prepare squash. Cut squash into chunks a little larger than the pieces of potato. Leave skin on if you like it (it is edible) or cut skin away with sharp knife.

3 Prepare onions. Peel away 1 or 2 outer layers, leaving a little of the root intact to hold onions together during roasting.

4 Place potatoes, squash and onions in a large pan, brush or rub with oil. Bake, uncovered, in 350°F oven about 1 hour or until browned and tender.

CAULIFLOWER AND BROCCOLI AU GRATIN

Important Points

- Cauliflower and broccoli are available all year round. Choose bright-colored broccoli with compact heads; avoid yellowing broccoli. Choose creamy white cauliflower with a tightly packed mass of flower buds (florets), surrounded by fresh green leaves. Store broccoli and cauliflower in the vegetable crisper in the refrigerator.

- When making the white sauce, stir the flour and butter over medium heat until bubbling to remove the raw taste of the flour. Stirring too long over the heat, however, will brown the flour and result in a brown sauce.

- Remove pan from heat before adding milk to prevent a lumpy sauce. If lumps do occur, use a small wire whisk to whisk sauce.

- It is important to boil the sauce, stirring constantly, for about 30 seconds after it thickens to give it a good shine.

- Recipe can be prepared several hours ahead and stored, covered, in the refrigerator.

- Suitable to freeze.

- Sauce, cauliflower and broccoli suitable to microwave.

You Need

¼ small (about 10oz) cauliflower
7oz broccoli
2 tablespoons (¼ stick) butter
3 tablespoons all-purpose flour
1½ cups milk
½ cup heavy cream
1 cup fresh bread crumbs
½ cup (2oz) grated cheddar cheese

1 Cut away thick stems from cauliflower and broccoli, break cauliflower and broccoli into small florets. Half fill a medium saucepan with water, bring to boil, add cauliflower, simmer, uncovered, 3 minutes. Add broccoli, simmer, uncovered, about 1 minute or until cauliflower and broccoli are just tender; drain in strainer.

2 Melt butter in a small saucepan, add flour, stir constantly over medium heat until bubbling. Remove the saucepan from heat, gradually stir in combined milk and cream, return the saucepan to medium heat, stir constantly until mixture boils and thickens.

3 Place cauliflower and broccoli into an ovenproof dish (5 cup capacity). Pour sauce over vegetables, stir gently to distribute sauce through vegetables.

4 Combine bread crumbs and cheese in a medium bowl. Sprinkle vegetables evenly with bread crumb mixture. Place the ovenproof dish on a baking sheet, bake, uncovered, in 350°F oven for about 20 minutes or until topping is golden brown.

■ MARINATED LAMB KABOBS WITH YOGURT SAUCE
■ TABBOULEH

Marinate the lamb cubes in this tasty mixture overnight to acquire flavor, then thread cubes onto skewers, cook and serve with tangy yogurt sauce and tabbouleh, a parsley salad. Serves 4.

SHOPPING LIST

4 medium (about 1½lb) lamb leg center slices
4 green onions
1 large (about ½lb) tomato
1 small (about 5oz) yellow bell pepper
fresh flat-leafed parsley
fresh mint
fresh oregano
garlic
4 large lemons
light olive oil
olive oil
dried oregano leaves
plain yogurt
tahini (sesame paste)
bulgur
chicken instant bouillon
4 pita pocket breads

WORK PLAN

1 Prepare lamb and marinade and combine; refrigerate.

2 Soak bulgur.

3 Prepare remaining ingredients for tabbouleh.

4 Drain bulgur and stir into remaining ingredients.

5 Drain lamb, thread onto skewers and cook.

6 Prepare yogurt sauce.

7 Serve marinated lamb kabobs immediately with yogurt sauce and tabbouleh, and pita pocket breads.

MARINATED LAMB KABOBS WITH YOGURT SAUCE

Important Points

- Lamb is at its best during spring. Store lamb in the meat keeper or in the coldest part of the refrigerator on a plate or a rack over a plate, loosely covered with baking paper, then plastic wrap or foil, allowing air to circulate around the meat.

- Use tender, lean cuts of lamb for kabobs; for example, shoulder, leg, loin.

- Kabobs can be pan-fried, broiled or barbequed. If pan-frying lamb that has been marinated, pat dry with absorbent paper before cooking to prevent oil from spitting.

- Rub oil onto metal skewers to stop meat sticking. Soak bamboo skewers in water for at least 1 hour or overnight, if time permits, to stop skewers burning.

- For flavor variety, a selection of fruit or vegetable pieces can be placed on skewers with lamb; for example, onion, mushroom, bell peppers, pineapple.

- Kabobs and yogurt sauce can be prepared a day ahead and stored, covered, in the refrigerator.

- Kabobs are best served immediately after cooking.

- Not suitable to freeze.

- Not suitable to microwave.

You Need

4 medium (about 1½lb) lamb leg center slices
3 tablespoons light olive oil
1 teaspoon dried oregano leaves

Marinade

½ cup light olive oil
¼ cup fresh lemon juice
1 teaspoon chicken instant bouillon
2 cloves garlic, minced
4 teaspoons chopped fresh oregano

Yogurt Sauce

3 tablespoons tahini (sesame paste)
2 teaspoons fresh lemon juice
½ cup plain yogurt
1 clove garlic, minced
3 tablespoons water

1 Trim as much fat as possible from lamb. Cut lamb into 1 inch cubes. Place lamb in a large bowl, add marinade, stir well, cover, refrigerate for 3 hours or overnight. Drain lamb from marinade, pat lamb dry with absorbent paper; discard marinade.

2 Thread lamb onto 8 skewers. Heat oil in a large skillet, add kabobs, 2 or 3 at a time, cook on both sides for about 5 minutes or until lamb is browned and tender (or broil or barbeque kabobs). Drain kabobs on absorbent paper. Sprinkle kabobs with dried oregano leaves before serving. Serve kabobs with yogurt sauce.

3 Marinade: Combine oil, lemon juice, instant bouillon, garlic and fresh oregano in a bowl, mix well.

4 Yogurt Sauce: Combine tahini and lemon juice in a bowl, stir in yogurt, garlic and water, cover, refrigerate.

TABBOULEH

Important Points

- Tabbouleh goes well with meat dishes, in pita pocket breads or hollowed-out bread rolls.
- Bulgur (cracked wheat) is available in natural food stores and some supermarkets. Store in an airtight container in a cool, dry place for up to 6 months.
- Bulgur needs no cooking, but is soaked in boiling water then drained and blotted on absorbent paper. Blot as much water as possible from bulgur for a chewy texture.
- You will need to buy about 2 large bunches of flat-leafed parsley (also known as Continental parsley) for this recipe.
- Chop parsley and mint as finely and evenly as possible; see Techniques section. You can use regular curly-leafed parsley if you prefer, but it tends to turn a little mushy and, of course, the flavor is different.
- Tabbouleh can be made 2 days ahead and stored, covered, in the refrigerator.
- Not suitable to freeze.

You Need

⅔ cup bulgur
4 green onions
1 large (about ½lb) tomato
1 small (about 5oz) yellow bell pepper
2 cups chopped fresh flat-leafed parsley
3 tablespoons chopped fresh mint
¼ cup olive oil
3 tablespoons fresh lemon juice

1 Place bulgur in a medium heatproof bowl, cover with boiling water, stand 15 minutes. While bulgur is soaking, chop onions and tomato. Cut pepper in half, remove stem, seeds and membrane; chop pepper.

2 Drain bulgur well in a fine strainer, rinse under cold water, drain well, blot moisture using absorbent paper or squeeze dry with your hand. Mix bulgur, onions, tomato, pepper, parsley, mint, oil and juice in a large bowl.

SALMON AND DILL QUICHE

Important Points

- Rich shortcrust pastry is one of the most used of all pastries for both savory and sweet pies, flans and tarts. See Techniques section before you start.

- Have all the ingredients cold for shortcrust pastry. If your hands are warm, rinse them under cold water and dry them before you start.

- The pastry should be handled quickly and lightly at all times; overhandling will make the pastry tough, dry and difficult to roll; see Techniques section.

- Use the minimum amount of liquid to bind the ingredients together. If pastry is too soft it will shrink during baking.

- Sifting the flour removes any lumps and incorporates air to give the pastry lightness.

- When rolling pastry, it is important to roll with an even pressure to help ensure an even thickness. Be careful not to roll over the edge. Roll the pastry with an up-and-down motion, turn the pastry clockwise, continue rolling up and down; do not roll from side to side.

- Refrigerate pastry for 30 minutes before rolling out and 30 minutes after lining the flan pan; this relaxes the pastry and helps prevent shrinkage during baking.

- Pastry is "baked blind" before the filling is added to ensure a crisp pastry case. You will need some dried beans or rice for this procedure.

- Serve with a green salad, if desired; see page 47.

- Salmon and dill quiche can be made a day ahead and stored, covered, in the refrigerator.

- Not suitable to freeze.

- Not suitable to microwave.

You Need

Rich Shortcrust Pastry

3oz (¾ stick) cold butter
1¼ cups (6oz) all-purpose flour
2 egg yolks
1 teaspoon cold water, approximately

Filling

8 green onions
2 teaspoons light olive oil
1 clove garlic, minced
7½oz can red salmon
¾ cup (3½oz) grated cheddar cheese
3 eggs
¾ cup milk
4 teaspoons chopped fresh dill

1 Rich Shortcrust Pastry: Cut cold butter into small pieces with a knife. Sift flour into a medium bowl, rub in butter quickly and gently with your fingertips (or process in a food processor until just combined). When the mixture looks like coarse bread crumbs – stop.

2 Add egg yolks and just enough water to make ingredients cling together. Mix the pastry with a knife until the mixture clings together in lumps, and then bring together lightly into a ball with the fingertips (this can be done in a food processor, using short pulse processing).

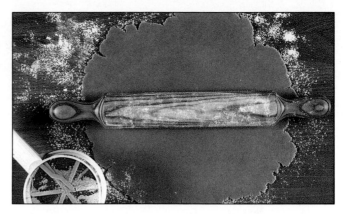

3 Turn pastry onto a lightly floured surface, gather and press any scraps and crumbs into the pastry, then use a "gather and press" motion with the fingertips until pastry is just smooth; use quick, light movements. Flatten pastry slightly, wrap in plastic wrap, refrigerate for 30 minutes.

4 Lightly grease a 9 inch flan pan. Roll the pastry on a lightly floured surface or between 2 sheets of baking paper into a circle large enough to line base and side of prepared pan. Roll the pastry in an up-and-down motion, turn the pastry clockwise, continue rolling up and down; do not roll over the edge.

5 Lift pastry gently over the rolling pin, lift into the flan pan. Do not stretch pastry. Ease pastry into the side of the pan with your fingers; trim pastry with a knife level with edge of flan pan. Prick base of pastry lightly with a fork. Refrigerate for 30 minutes.

6 To "bake blind", cover pastry with baking paper. Place about 1½ cups dried beans or rice into pastry case. Place flan pan on a baking sheet, bake in 375°F oven for 10 minutes. Carefully lift paper with beans from pastry case. Bake pastry case for about 10 more minutes or until pastry is lightly browned; cool.

7 Filling: Chop onions finely. Heat oil in a small saucepan, add onions and garlic, cook, stirring, until onions are soft but not colored. Spread onion mixture evenly into pastry case. Drain salmon, remove bones and any black skin. Flake salmon, sprinkle evenly over onion mixture; sprinkle evenly with half the cheese.

8 Combine eggs, milk and dill in a large jug, mix with a wire whisk or fork, pour over salmon mixture; sprinkle evenly with remaining cheese. Bake, uncovered, in 350°F oven for about 45 minutes or until filling is firm and lightly browned.

■ VEAL WITH SOUR CREAM AND PAPRIKA

■ HERBED RICE

It's important to have the skillet very hot when you're frying the strips of veal steak, otherwise the veal will toughen. For the rice, we've used the boiling method; remember to add the rice very slowly to the boiling water and it will be light and fluffy, like ours. Serves 2.

SHOPPING LIST

10oz veal steak
1 small (about 2½oz) onion
½ small (about 2½oz) green bell pepper
3½oz button mushrooms
fresh chives
fresh basil
1 lemon
all-purpose flour
light olive oil
butter
sour cream
paprika
Worcestershire sauce
tomato paste
chicken broth
white long-grain rice

WORK PLAN

1 Prepare veal and vegetables.

2 Put water on for rice.

3 Cook veal.

4 Put rice on to cook.

5 Cook vegetables for veal, add sauce, juice, paste and broth.

6 Strain rice.

7 Add veal and sour cream to pan.

8 Heat butter, add rice and herbs.

9 Serve veal with sour cream sond paprika, and herbed rice.

VEAL WITH SOUR CREAM AND PAPRIKA

Important Points

- Veal should be pale pink with little or no fat.
- Store veal in the meat keeper or in the coldest part of the refrigerator on a plate or a rack over a plate, loosely covered with baking paper, then plastic wrap or foil, allowing air to circulate around the veal.
- Veal is lean and tender and does not have a strong flavor of its own. It goes well with a strong-flavored sauce.
- It is important that the veal be sealed (see Terms section) in the initial stages of cooking in this recipe. The skillet should be very hot and the veal cooked in batches. Too much veal in the pan will reduce the temperature of the skillet and cause the veal to stew and be tough.
- Chicken broth can be made with a bouillon cube or instant bouillon, or you can make chicken broth; see page 121.
- Mushrooms are available all year round. Choose firm, dry, clean, undamaged mushrooms.
- Store mushrooms, unwashed, in a brown paper or calico bag in the refrigerator for 3 to 5 days.
- Brush or wipe mushrooms with a damp cloth; do not wash or peel.
- Recipe can be prepared a day ahead; add sour cream just before serving.
- Not suitable to freeze.
- Not suitable to microwave.

You Need

10oz veal steak
1 small (about 2½oz) onion
½ small (about 2½oz) green bell pepper
3½oz button mushrooms
4 teaspoons light olive oil
1 tablespoon butter
2 teaspoons all-purpose flour
1 teaspoon paprika
½ teaspoon Worcestershire sauce
1 teaspoon fresh lemon juice
2 teaspoons tomato paste
½ cup chicken broth
½ cup sour cream

1 Cut veal into thin strips. Chop onion finely; see Techniques section. Remove stem, seeds and membrane from pepper, chop pepper finely. Wipe mushrooms and slice thinly. Heat oil and butter in a large skillet over high heat until butter is bubbling. Add veal in batches, cook until well browned and sealed, remove from skillet with tongs. Transfer to a heatproof plate.

2 Reheat the skillet, add onion and pepper, cook, stirring, until onion is soft. Add mushrooms, cook, stirring, until mushrooms are tender.

3 Add flour and paprika to the skillet, stir until combined. Remove the skillet from heat, stir in combined Worcestershire sauce, lemon juice, tomato paste and chicken broth. Return the skillet to heat, stir constantly until mixture boils and thickens. Reduce heat, simmer, uncovered, for 5 minutes.

4 Return veal and any juices to the skillet, stir until combined. Add sour cream, stir constantly over medium heat, without boiling, or until heated through.

HERBED RICE

Important Points

- In this recipe we are cooking rice by the boiling method.
- There are several varieties and types of rice. Short-grain and long-grain white rice will take between 10 to 15 minutes to cook by the boiling method. Brown rice will take from 25 to 30 minutes.
- Add rice gradually to the saucepan of boiling water. If you drop it in all at once, the water will go off the boil, the rice will stick to the bottom of the pan and be gluey.
- If you want to use rice for a salad, spread it out on absorbent paper or a kitchen towel to drain and dry thoroughly.
- Rice can be boiled 2 days ahead and stored, covered, in refrigerator.
- Suitable to freeze.
- Rice is suitable to microwave but takes about the same time as it does by conventional cooking methods.

You Need

⅔ cup white long-grain rice
2 tablespoons (¼ stick) butter
4 teaspoons chopped fresh chives
4 teaspoons chopped fresh basil

1 Two-thirds fill a medium saucepan with water. Cover the saucepan, bring to the boil over high heat, sprinkle rice gradually into boiling water. Boil rice rapidly, uncovered, for about 10 minutes or until just tender. Do not over-cook rice; test rice by biting a few grains.

2 Tip rice into a strainer and drain well. Melt butter in the saucepan, return rice to the saucepan, stir herbs in lightly over medium heat until heated through.

CRISP FRIED FISH

Important Points

- Fish should be eaten as soon as possible after purchase. If not eaten immediately, fish should be wrapped and stored in an airtight container in the coldest part of the refrigerator for up to 2 days.
- When choosing fish, feel the fish, if possible; the flesh should feel firm to the touch.
- Fish should not smell unpleasant.
- Ensure that the skin of the fish is not dry, and that there are no traces of discoloration.
- If possible, bring fish to room temperature before cooking.
- Small whole fish, fillets, cutlets and steaks can be deep-fried. Cooking time will depend on thickness of the fish.
- Use a wide-topped deep-fryer, preferably with a heavy base. Never cover the fryer with a lid.
- We use a wire frying basket for safety and convenience when lowering food into hot oil and lifting it out again. You can also use a slotted metal spoon or tongs, but always be careful when cooking with hot oil.
- Never leave frying foods unattended; overheated oil can catch fire.
- We use good-quality all-purpose oil for deep-frying; read the label to check suitability.
- The deep-fryer should be only half full of oil; excessive oil is wasteful and dangerous. The amount of oil used will vary with the size of the fryer.
- Heat oil for deep-frying; to test heat, see Techniques section.
- Cook only 1 or 2 pieces of fish at a time, depending on the size of the deep-fryer; it must not be overcrowded. Adding too much at a time lowers the temperature of the oil and fish will not be crisp.
- Serve crisp fried fish immediately. Serve with lemon wedges to squeeze over fish, if desired; the juice gives the fish a flavor boost and cuts down any oily taste.
- Not suitable to freeze.
- Not suitable to microwave.

You Need

4 (about 1¼lb) firm white fish fillets
coarse (kosher) salt
¼ cup cornstarch
oil for deep-frying

Batter
1 cup (5oz) self-rising flour
1 cup water, approximately

1 To remove skin from fillets, place fillets skin-side-down onto a board. Take a good pinch of salt in your fingers, hold tip of fillet down firmly with salty fingers; the salt helps you get a firm grip. Using a sharp knife, held almost flat against board, use a "press and push" action carefully to separate flesh from skin.

2 Dust fish fillets with cornstarch, shake away excess cornstarch. Using tongs, dip fish into batter to coat fish all over. Allow excess batter to drain from fish.

3 Half fill a large, deep-fryer with oil. Heat oil; see Techniques. Place fish into wire frying basket; lower basket into oil, deep-fry fish until cooked, lift from oil; drain.

4 Batter: Sift flour into a medium bowl. Using a wire whisk, gradually beat in enough water to give a smooth pouring consistency.

POTATO FRIES

Important Points

- Choose firm, well-shaped potatoes, free from blemishes, cuts and sprouts, and with few eyes. Avoid green potatoes.
- Store potatoes in a cool, dry, dark place with good ventilation.
- The double-fry method of cooking potato fries will give the best results. After the first fry, the temperature of the oil will drop. Reheat the oil and fry the potato fries until tender. To test the heat of the oil, see Techniques section.
- If preparing potato fries ahead of time, keep cut potatoes covered with cold water in a bowl until ready for cooking. This prevents discoloration and removes excess starch which tends to make the fries stick together.
- Potato fries can be prepared and fried for the first time 1 hour ahead. The second frying must be done just before serving.
- Not suitable to freeze.
- Not suitable to microwave.

You Need

4 large (about 1½lb) old potatoes
oil for deep-frying

1 Peel potatoes; remove any "eyes" with the point of a sharp knife. Cut potatoes into½ inch slices then into ½ inch strips or finer, if desired. Place fries in a large bowl and cover with cold water until ready to use. Drain fries in strainer. Dry fries thoroughly with a kitchen towel or on absorbent paper before frying.

2 Half fill a large, deep-fryer with oil. Heat oil; see Techniques. Place fries into wire frying basket; lower gradually so oil won't splatter. Deep-fry for a few minutes, lift from oil in basket. Drain fries on absorbent paper. Reheat oil; return fries to basket, deep-fry again until golden brown. Drain on absorbent paper.

COLESLAW

Important Points

- Choose firm, crisp cabbage, heavy for its size, with fresh, bright-colored outer leaves.
- Store cabbage in vegetable crisper or in refrigerator in a plastic bag, wrapped in a paper towel to absorb moisture.
- You can use any type of cabbage; the traditional one is the firm white round-head cabbage.
- Mayonnaise can be made in a bowl or in a blender or food processor.
- If the mayonnaise curdles, it is usually because the oil is added too quickly. If this happens, transfer the curdled mixture from the bowl (blender or food processor) to a jug. Place another egg yolk into the bowl (blender or food processor), add the curdled mixture drop by drop, beating all the time. Once the mixture is holding together, add the rest of the curdled mixture in a thin stream, beating all the time.
- Coleslaw can be made 3 days ahead and stored, covered, in the refrigerator.
- Not suitable to freeze.

You Need

½ medium (about 1½lb) cabbage
1 medium (about ¼lb) carrot
4 green onions

Mayonnaise
2 egg yolks
1 teaspoon dry mustard
2 teaspoons fresh lemon juice
1 cup salad oil
3 tablespoons milk, approximately

1 Remove core and outer leaves from cabbage. Shred cabbage finely. Peel and grate carrot. Chop onions.

2 Combine cabbage, carrot, onions and mayonnaise in a large bowl; mix well.

3 Mayonnaise: Combine yolks and mustard in a medium bowl, beat well with a wire whisk (or blend or process egg yolks, mustard and juice until smooth).

4 Add oil, drop by drop, beating all the time. Mixture should be thick by the time half the oil is added. Beat in juice, then beat in remaining oil gradually. Add enough milk to give consistency desired.

114

PANTRY GUIDE

Here we have listed the basic ingredients used many times in our recipes, as well as a few extras that you might need. If you have a selection on hand, it will make preparing these meals even easier. All you will then need to do is buy in fresh foods such as meat, poultry, seafood, fruit and vegetables before you start to cook.

ALCOHOL
Brandy
Dry red wine
Dry white wine
Port wine
Sherry: dry and sweet

BREAD CRUMBS
Fresh
Packaged unseasoned

CANNED PRODUCTS
Anchovy fillets
Baby carrots
Baked beans
Beets
Coconut cream, unsweetened
Coconut milk, unsweetened
Corn: creamed, whole-kernel
Garbanzo beans
Potatoes
Red kidney beans
Salmon
Three-bean mix
Tomatoes
Tuna
White kidney beans (cannellini)

CONDIMENTS, ETC.
Black pepper
Bouillon cubes: beef, chicken, vegetable
Bouillon, instant: beef, chicken
Capers
Celery salt
Chutney
Coarse (kosher) salt
Curry powder
Dill pickles
Garlic
Garlic salt
Herb and garlic dressing
Horseradish cream
Jelly: mint, red currant
Lemon pepper seasoning
Mayonnaise
Mustard: dry, French, seeded
Olives, black, green
Peanut butter
Sambal oelek
Tahini (sesame paste)
Tomato paste
Tomato puree

EGGS
2oz

DAIRY PRODUCE
Butter
Cheese: cheddar, cream cheese, jarlsberg, Parmesan
Cream: sour, heavy
Ghee

FLOUR
All-purpose flour
Cornmeal
Cornmeal, yellow
Cornstarch
Self-rising flour

FROZEN PRODUCTS
Mixed vegetables
Peas
Spinach

FRUIT, CANNED
Apricots
Peaches
Pears
Pineapple

FRUIT, DRIED
Raisins, dark seedless
Raisins, golden

HERBS, DRIED
Marjoram
Mint
Mixed
Oregano
Parsley
Rosemary
Tarragon
Thyme

JAM, ETC.
Honey
Marmalade

JUICES
Apple
Apricot
Orange

NUTS
Almonds, sliced
Pine nuts
Unsalted roasted cashews
Unsalted roasted peanuts
Walnuts

OILS & FATS
Beef dripping
Light olive
Olive
Salad

PASTA
Fettuccine
Lasagne
Penne
Shells
Spaghetti

PASTRY, ETC.
Corn chips
Pappadams
Phyllo pastry
Ready-rolled puff pastry
Ready-rolled shortcrust pastry

RICE AND PULSES
Bulgur (cracked wheat)
Lentils
Rice: white: long-grain, short-grain; brown

SAUCES
Chili
Hoisin
Oyster-flavored
Plum
Soy: light and dark
Sweet and sour
Tabasco
Worcestershire

SPICES
All-spice
Caraway seeds
Cardamom pods
Chili flakes
Chili powder
Cinnamon sticks
Cuminseed
Garam masala
Mixed spice
Nutmeg
Paprika
Saffron: ground and threads
Seasoned pepper

SUGAR
Brown, dark
Granulated
Superfine

TOMATO
Canned whole tomatoes
Ketchup
Puree
Tomato paste

VINEGAR
Brown
Cider
Red wine
White
White wine

EQUIPMENT

Throughout this book, we used easily obtainable equipment and have pictured it here so you will know what we mean when we specify various items. Good equipment certainly helps you to cook well, but we don't suggest you buy everything at once; simply acquire various bits and pieces as you progress.

1. MEASURING CUPS AND SPOONS: see information panel on page 126.

2. APPLE CORER: makes removing apple cores so easy; choose one with a strong, rigid blade.

3. ROASTING PAN: choose a heavy, deep-sided pan. Some roasting pans have lids, but foil can be used to cover pans when necessary.

4. BOWLS: a selection of small, medium and large bowls is useful. We've pictured glass bowls, but other types of bowls are suitable.

5. BRUSHES: pastry brushes are useful; 2 brushes are a good buy. Use one for brushing oil, butter, egg, etc., and another for brushing flour from pastry, egg-washing pastry, brushing meats with marinades etc.

6. CAN OPENER: choose a well-made, strong can opener; may be hand-operated or electric.

7. CHOPPING BOARD: choose a large, thick, wooden board made of hard wood. Wash well after each use.

8. COLANDER: a very large strainer.

9. EGG-SLICE: for turning large items during cooking.

10. FOOD PROCESSOR: choose a solid machine with a large work bowl and strong motor. Look for a processor with a variety of blades and attachments.

11. FRYING BASKET: makes it easier to lower and raise food out of hot oil; for example, potato fries.

12. SKILLETS: small, medium, large; choose heavy skillets. Recipes sometimes require a skillet with a lid.

13. GARLIC MINCER: useful for mincing small quantities of garlic. We prefer to use a knife. See Mincing Garlic in Techniques section.

14. GRATER: choose a hand-held box-shaped grater for general purposes.

15. JUGS: small, medium, large. Choose heatproof measuring jugs.

16. JUICER: a plastic juicer with a container underneath to catch the juice is the most useful type to choose.

17. KITCHEN SCISSORS: use large, good-quality scissors with heavy blades.

18. KNIFE, FORK, SPOON: your kitchen cutlery will do. Metal spoons can be handy for mixing and serving.

19. KNIVES: the 3 most useful are a large chef's knife for chopping, a small paring knife for peeling and trimming, and a serrated knife for slicing bread. Other sizes are also useful; you will soon find your favorites. Choose good-quality, heavy knives.

20. MEAT POUNDER: for flattening and tenderizing meat and poultry.

21. MUFFIN TINS: useful for muffins and little pies; available in different sizes.

22. OVENPROOF DISHES: choose different-sized casserole dishes, with or without a lid, to meet your needs.

23. BAKING SHEET: a flat tray, often with sides ½ inch high.

24. PALLET KNIFE: large and small; used for lifting and spreading.

25. PASTA TONGS: for lifting and serving pasta.

26. PEPPER GRINDER: used for freshly ground black pepper.

27. DEEP-DISH PIE PLATE: ovenproof dish suitable for pies both savory and sweet.

28. POTATO MASHER: used for coarsely mashing a variety of foods.

29. POULTRY SHEARS: easier than a knife for cutting poultry into sections (or use kitchen scissors).

30. ROLLING PIN: choose a wooden rolling pin with easy-to-grip handles for rolling large areas of pastry evenly; should be easy to wipe clean.

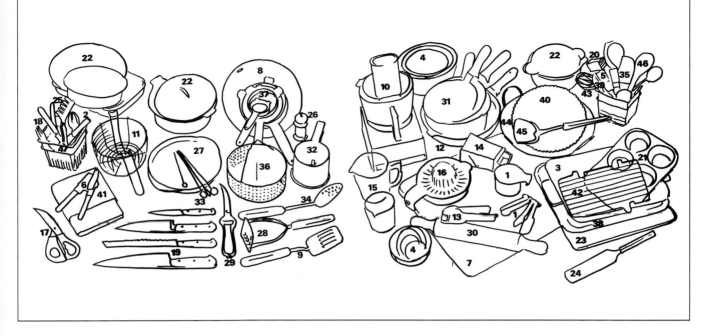

31. SAUCEPANS: small, medium, large. Saucepans should be deep and straight-sided to maintain the heat. Choose saucepans with a heavy base, tight-fitting lid and securely attached handle.

32. SIFTER: for aerating dry ingredients.

33. SKEWERS: can be metal or bamboo; large skewers can be used for threading with meat, chicken, etc., for kabobs. A fine skewer is ideal for testing if meat and poultry are cooked. You can also test cakes, etc., with a skewer.

34. SLOTTED SPOON: rounded base holds food while liquid drains back into saucepan or dish, etc.

35. SPATULA: a flexible rubber blade on a wooden handle for scraping pans and bowls.

36. STEAMING BASKET: either metal or bamboo.

37. STRAINERS: a large strainer with fine mesh allows you to drain large quantities easily; many sizes are available for different purposes.

38. JELLY-ROLL PAN: a shallow rectangular pan with many uses.

39. TONGS: useful for lifting and turning hot foods of many kinds; best for turning steaks and chops, etc., when a fork would pierce the meat and allow juices to run out. When choosing tongs, make sure the ends meet.

40: 9 INCH FLAN PAN: a metal flan pan conducts heat well and bakes pastry evenly. Choose one with a removable base.

41. WEIGHING SCALES: choose easy-to-read scales.

42. WIRE RACK: to elevate foods off the base of pan during broiling and roasting. Also for cooling cakes, cookies, etc.

43. WIRE WHISK: choose a variety of sizes. A small, flattened whisk is suitable for making sauces, a balloon-shaped whisk is suitable for whisking ingredients together.

44. WOK: for stir-frying.

45. WOK SPOON (wok chan): for stir-frying; shaped to suit the shape of a wok.

46. WOODEN SPOONS: come in all shapes and sizes; choose a variety.

47. VEGETABLE PEELER: choose a sturdy swivel-blade peeler.

TECHNIQUES

We use these methods all the time in our Test Kitchen as they are so simple and efficient. They are easy for you to carry out, too. You'll find they streamline procedures and also give you a valuable range of skills.

PREPARING ASPARAGUS

First, snap off the fibrous ends of the asparagus spears. To find the snapping point, bend the spear a little and the end should snap off easily; each spear has a slightly different snapping point. Then scrape away the little nodules from the ends (not the tips) of the spears; we use a vegetable peeler to do this.

PREPARING AVOCADOS

Prepare avocados close to serving time because they discolor rapidly. Dip cut avocado pieces into fresh lemon juice to help prevent discoloration.

To remove an avocado seed:
Cut all the way around the avocado with a sharp knife, cutting through to the seed. Twist the avocado into 2 pieces. Hold the half with the seed in 1 hand, hit the seed lightly but sharply with the knife blade and twist knife; the seed should slip out easily. Occasionally, a seed is not as hard as others, so don't hit with force in case you cut right through the seed and cut your hand. Alternatively, place the half avocado on a chopping board when you hit the seed with the knife. If using only half an avocado, leave seed in place in 1 half, wrap tightly in plastic wrap and refrigerate for up to 2 days.

To peel an avocado:
Cut the avocado in half and remove the seed. Hold the half avocado in 1 hand and peel away the skin. Some varieties of avocado are difficult to peel, and you may need a knife to remove the skin.

To slice an avocado:
Cut the avocado in half and remove the seed. Place half on a chopping board and slice from the middle, as shown, or from the side.

MAKING BREAD CRUMBS

Where fresh bread crumbs are specified, use 1 to 2-day-old white or whole-wheat bread. Do not use very fresh bread because the crumbs will be soggy. Remove crusts from bread; discard crusts. Cut or break bread into pieces, blend or process until fine crumbs form. Store bread crumbs in an airtight container or in plastic bags. Bread crumbs can be frozen.

TO SEPARATE EGGS

A recipe may specify that egg yolks and egg whites are used separately, or you may need only the egg yolk or the egg white for a recipe.

Crack shell by tapping gently on a flat surface or sharp edge, preferably not the mixing bowl. Break the shell in half and "see-saw" the yolk between shell halves to allow the white to run into a bowl. It is a good idea to break each egg separately into a separate small bowl so you can see that the egg is fresh before adding it to the other eggs.

GRATING CHEESE, GINGERROOT AND ZEST

When necessary, recipes will indicate if a food needs to be coarsely or finely grated; use the appropriate sized area on the grater. Here are 3 examples; take care not to grate your fingers!

To grate cheese:
If a recipe specifies a quantity of grated cheese, cut that quantity off the piece and grate it; otherwise, grate as required to make half a cup or a tablespoon, etc.

To grate fresh gingerroot:
Peel or scrape away skin with a vegetable knife and grate gingerroot as required.

To grate citrus zest:
Grate only the colored part of the peel because the white pith of citrus fruit is quite bitter. We use a pastry brush to brush grated zest from outside and inside the grater.

MINCING GARLIC

Use a garlic mincer for odor-free fingers. Place peeled clove (broken away from the knob) in the mincer, press down with top half of mincer. Scrape off with a knife.

To mince garlic with a knife:
Peel a clove, slice it on a chopping board with a tiny pinch of salt. Using the broad part of a knife blade, mash garlic by pushing the knife away from you.

TO TEST HEAT OF OIL

When shallow-frying or deep-frying, use a tasteless vegetable oil that can be heated to the required temperature without burning. Some foods are lightly deep-fried; others need higher heat. You'll need to experiment, but be careful with hot oil so you don't burn yourself. Never leave frying foods unattended. Here we show the test with deep-frying; the same test suits shallow-frying.

1. At a lower temperature, a gentle fizz is produced if a piece of bread is added.

2. At a higher temperature, the bread will fizz vigorously and begin to brown.

PREPARING GHEE

Ghee is a pure butter fat available in supermarkets (see Glossary), but it's easy to prepare at home. The process is also known as clarifying butter.

1. Heat butter in a saucepan until it is melted and becomes frothy. Remove foam with a spoon.

2. Pour butter into a heatproof bowl; discard solid bits and pieces in saucepan. Cool ghee, cover, refrigerate.

SLICING LEEKS

First trim away the tough green leaves and the root end; use only the white leek leaves. Leeks usually contain grit, so cut in half lengthways and wash and dry carefully so the leaves don't fall apart.

1. Cutting horizontal slices.

2. Cutting fine strips.

CHOPPING HERBS

Place washed and dried sprigs or leaves on a chopping board. Using a sharp knife, hold knife tip down and "rock" the knife over the herb.

PREPARING ONIONS

First, peel away the tough outer layers. Trim root end but leave root intact to help hold onions together during chopping.

To chop an onion:

1. Cut onion in half lengthways. Place half cut-side-down on a chopping board. Hold onion as shown, cut lengthways as finely as possible without cutting right through to the root end.

2. Cut onion horizontally almost through to the root end. If onion is large, 2 or 3 cuts are necessary.

3. Cut across onion as finely as required; discard root end.

To slice an onion:

1. Hold onion as shown, slice as finely as required; discard root end.

PASTRY TIPS

To rub in butter:

Butter should be cold; chop butter. Sift flour into a bowl, add butter. Pick up a few small pieces of butter and plenty of flour between fingertips and thumbs. Gently but quickly rub the butter into the flour, squashing the butter lightly as you do so. Shake the bowl so the unrubbed pieces of butter come to the top. When the mixture looks like very coarse bread crumbs, stop; don't overhandle the crumbs.

To roll out pastry:

Always cover pastry and refrigerate for at least 30 minutes before rolling, unless otherwise specified. Divide a large amount of pastry into 2 or more pieces for easy rolling. Here are 2 ways to roll pastry.

1. Place the pastry on a smooth surface lightly sprinkled with flour. Flatten pastry into a smooth round with your fingertips. With a rolling pin, roll from the center to the edge; not over the edge. Sprinkle a little more flour over the surface if the pastry sticks; do not use too much flour as this unbalances the proportions of the other ingredients. Use an up-and-down motion, turn the pastry clockwise, continue rolling up and down, don't roll from side to side. Roll pastry to an even thickness to prevent shrinkage during cooking.

2. Another way is to place the pastry

round between baking paper or plastic wrap and roll as described. There's no need to use flour.

To pinch a frill around pastry:

Trim pastry edge with a knife, then push edge against thumb and finger, as shown.

To make pastry leaves:

Using a sharp knife, cut leaf shapes; decorate leaves with the back of the knife.

TO PEEL AND SEED TOMATOES

To peel and seed a tomato:

1. Remove stem end from tomatoes with the point of a sharp knife.

2. Place tomatoes in a large heatproof bowl, cover with boiling water, stand for about 30 seconds or until skins begin to lift.

3. Transfer tomatoes to a large bowl of cold water, stand for about 30 seconds or until cool enough to handle. Skins should peel away easily.

4. Cut tomatoes in half, scrape seeds out carefully with a teaspoon.

TESTING STEAK

It can be difficult to determine the stage at which steak is ready to be served; experience is the best teacher. Check if people like steak well-cooked, medium or barely cooked (rare), also known as blue.

1. Tenderloin steak, from left, is rare; medium; and well done.

2. Steak cooked to the rare stage is quite spongy and soft to the touch, as shown. Medium is less spongy and so on.

HOW TO HEAT DINNER PLATES

Food to be eaten hot should always be served on hot plates. To avoid damage, never overheat plates. You can heat plates in several different ways.

● Place them in a 300°F oven for about 15 minutes. Or, if your stove has a broiler above the oven, it will probably be hot enough from the heat of the oven to warm the plates there; simply place them in the broiler compartment for about 15 minutes or until warmed.

● Some stoves have a warming oven or drawers for warming plates; check the manufacturer's manual for instructions.

● Plates can also be warmed by standing them in a sink of very hot water for a few minutes until you need them; dry plates thoroughly before using.

● Plates can also be heated in a microwave oven by placing pieces of damp absorbent paper between the plates (remember, silver or gold-trimmed plates cannot be used in microwave ovens as the metal content causes "arcing" and possible damage to the oven). First of all check the manufacturer's manual for instructions.

MAKE YOUR OWN BROTH

BEEF BROTH

4lb meaty beef bones
2 onions
2 stalks celery, chopped
2 carrots, chopped
3 bay leaves
2 teaspoons black peppercorns
20 cups water
12 cups water, extra

Place bones and unpeeled chopped onions in roasting pan. Bake, uncovered, in 400°F oven about 1 hour or until bones and onions are well browned. Transfer bones and onions to large pan, add celery, carrots, bay leaves, peppercorns and water, simmer, uncovered, 3 hours. Add extra water, simmer, uncovered, further 1 hour; strain.

Makes about 10 cups.

■ Broth can be made 4 days ahead.
■ Storage: Covered, in refrigerator.
■ Freeze: Suitable.
■ Microwave: Not suitable.

CHICKEN BROTH

4lb chicken bones
2 onions, chopped
2 stalks celery, chopped
2 carrots, chopped
3 bay leaves
2 teaspoons black peppercorns
20 cups water

Combine all ingredients in large pan, simmer, uncovered, 2 hours; strain.

Makes about 10 cups.

■ Broth can be made 4 days ahead.
■ Storage: Covered, in refrigerator.
■ Freeze: Suitable.
■ Microwave: Not suitable.

FISH BROTH

3lb fish bones
12 cups water
1 onion, chopped
2 stalks celery, chopped
2 bay leaves
1 teaspoon black peppercorns

Combine all ingredients in large pan, simmer, uncovered, 20 minutes; strain.

Makes about 10 cups.

■ Broth can be made 4 days ahead.
■ Storage: Covered, in refrigerator.
■ Freeze: Suitable.
■ Microwave: Not suitable.

VEGETABLE BROTH

1 large carrot, chopped
1 large parsnip, chopped
2 onions, chopped
6 stalks celery, chopped
4 bay leaves
2 teaspoons black peppercorns
12 cups water

Combine all ingredients in large pan, simmer, uncovered, 1½ hours; strain.

Makes about 5 cups.

■ Broth can be made 4 days ahead.
■ Storage: Covered, in refrigerator.
■ Freeze: Suitable.
■ Microwave: Not suitable.

TERMS

In 1 or 2 words, cooking "shorthand" can tell you many things about the procedures to follow in a recipe; it's fascinating to learn them. Here are some of the most common terms we have used in this book.

AL DENTE: an Italian term generally applied to the cooking of pasta. Translated it means "to the tooth", meaning pasta should be firm when bitten, not soft.

BAKE BLIND: a term used when baking a pastry case without a filling. Some recipes require the pastry case to be pricked lightly with a fork to keep the pastry case flat; follow individual recipes. Line pastry case with baking paper, fill cavity with dried beans or rice. Bake as recipe directs. Towards the end of cooking time, remove beans or rice and paper, return pastry case to oven to complete cooking.

BASTE: to spoon over liquid (usually fat, oil, broth or pan juices) during cooking to prevent food from drying out; for example, roasted meat and kabobs.

BLANCH: commonly used to mean precook or parboil (partly cook) vegetables for a short time so they need little or no further cooking.

BOIL: to cook in liquid at boiling point; boiling point of water is 212°F.

BRAISE: food (generally meat and/or vegetables) cooked, covered, in very little liquid. Meat and vegetables are browned first, then liquid added.

BROIL: a method of cooking by exposing food to dry heat. The heat can come from a variety of sources: gas or electric stove broiler, red coals of barbeque or outdoor fire, surface of griddle pan heated on stove or over an open fire.

DEEP-FRY: to cook in a deep, heavy-based deep-fryer or pan in sufficient fat or oil to cover food completely. Used for foods that take a short time to cook such as fish fillets, potato fries and fritters.

DEGLAZE: to heat liquid (usually broth and/or wine) in a dish or pan so that the sediment left after roasting or frying forms a sauce with the liquid.

DEGORGE: to extract juices from meat, fish or vegetables, generally by salting then soaking or rinsing. Usually done to remove excessive moisture or strong-tasting juices.

GREASE PANS, ETC: use melted butter applied with a brush, or appropriate sprays, if preferred.

JULIENNE: vegetables or citrus peel cut into thin matchsticks or very fine shreds. Turkey, chicken, ham, etc., can also be cut into julienne strips for inclusion in a salad.

MARINADE: seasoned mixture generally of oil and wine, with herbs and other flavorings, used to stand (marinate) meat or fish in for some hours or overnight before cooking. This gives flavor and sometimes tenderizes the food.

REDUCE: to boil a mixture, uncovered, until the quantity is reduced and the flavor concentrated.

REFRESH: applies to cooked foods, mainly vegetables, which are drained and then passed quickly under cold water to stop the cooking process and help preserve color.

RELAX (of pastry): to set aside pastry in a cool place - usually the refrigerator, for about 30 minutes - after rolling out. In the rolling process, the gluten (or protein in flour) expands, and it needs resting time to contract. This lessens the possibility that the pastry will shrink during cooking.

ROUX: most sauces start with a roux, a mixture of melted butter and flour. There are 3 kinds of roux, ranging from white to brown. The color is simply determined by the length of cooking time.

SAUTE: a term applied to food cooked quickly in a shallow skillet. The food must be completely dry before putting into the hot fat; do not crowd the pan or the food will not brown well.

SEAL: to brown meat quickly on both sides to hold the juices; the heat is usually then lowered for the remainder of the cooking time.

SHALLOW-FRY: to cook in a small quantity of fat or oil in a shallow pan. Used for foods which take a comparatively long time to cook, such as sausages, crumbed cutlets, thick pieces of fish or whole fish.

SIMMER: to bring food in liquid to the boil, then to reduce heat and keep the food cooking slowly, just below boiling point, at about 180°F. A method of cooking suitable for casseroles and similar dishes which need long, slow cooking.

STEAM: to cook food in the steam from boiling water. A flexible metal steamer with perforations which fits inside a saucepan is excellent for vegetables or fish. Bamboo steamers are also useful for certain foods.

STIR-FRY: ingredients are cooked quickly over high heat in a wok, and are stir-fried or tossed constantly using a wok spoon (wok chan) which is specially shaped to suit the wok. A skillet can be used.

SWEAT: to cook food gently in butter or oil in a covered pan or skillet over very low heat. Generally used for vegetables, particularly onions. The slow cooking extracts flavor.

GLOSSARY

Here are some names, terms and alternatives to help everyone understand and use our recipes perfectly.

ALCOHOL: is optional, but gives a particular flavor. Use fruit juice or water instead to make up the liquid content required, if preferred.

ALMONDS:
Sliced: thinly sliced almonds.

BAKING PAPER: can be used to line baking pans and make paper cones for piping, etc. It is not necessary to grease this paper after lining pans.

BAMBOO SKEWERS: can be used instead of metal skewers if soaked in water overnight or for several hours beforehand to prevent burning during cooking. They are available in several different lengths.

BEEF:
Boneless beef chuck: a forequarter cut.
Corned beef: cut from the outside of the upper leg and cured.
Ground beef: we used lean ground beef.
Rib eye steak: cut from eye of rib roast.
Sirloin: steak with or without a bone.

BEEF DRIPPING: animal fat; use oil if preferred.

BEETS: regular round beets. The beet leaves can also be used.

BREAD CRUMBS:
Packaged unseasoned: use fine. packaged unseasoned bread crumbs.
Fresh: use 1 or 2-day-old bread made into crumbs by grating, blending or processing (see Techniques section).

BROTH: 1 cup broth is the equivalent of 1 cup water plus 1 crumbled bouillon cube (or 1 teaspoon instant bouillon). If you prefer to make your own fresh broth, see recipes on page 121.

BUTTER: use salted or unsalted butter.

CAPERS: pickled buds of a Mediterranean shrub used as a flavoring.

CARAWAY SEEDS: a member of the parsley family, caraway is available in seed or ground form. Pictured on page 124.

CARDAMOM: an expensive spice with an exotic fragrance. It can be bought in pod, seed or ground form. You can grind cardamom from the seeds in a mortar and pestle.

Clockwise from top: Cardamom pods; cardamom seeds; ground cardamom.

CASHEWS: we used unsalted roasted cashews available from natural food stores and most supermarkets.

CHEESE:
Cheddar: we used a firm, good-tasting cheddar.
Jarlsberg: a Norwegian cheese made from cows' milk; has large holes and a mild, nutty taste.

Parmesan: sharp-tasting cheese used as a flavor accent. We prefer to use fresh Parmesan cheese, although it is also available already finely grated.

CHILI PEPPERS: are available in many different types and sizes. Small ones (birds' eye or bird peppers) are the hottest. Use tight rubber gloves when chopping fresh chili peppers as they can burn your skin.
Flakes, dried: available at Asian food stores.
Powder: the Asian variety is the hottest and is made from ground chili peppers. It can be used as a substitute for fresh chili peppers in the proportions of ½ teaspoon chili powder to 1 medium chopped fresh chili pepper.

Clockwise from left: Dried red chili peppers; large fresh chili peppers; small (birds' eye) chili peppers; dried chili flakes; chili powder.

CHILI SAUCE: we used a hot Chinese variety. It consists of chili peppers, salt and vinegar. We used it sparingly; you can increase it to suit your taste.

CILANTRO: also known as Chinese parsley; it is essential to many south-east Asian cuisines. Use it sparingly until you are accustomed to the flavor. The leaves, stems and roots can be used. Pictured overpage.

Clockwise from top: Fresh cilantro; ground coriander; coriander seeds.

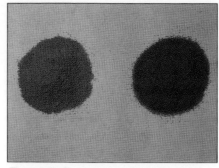

From left: Cornmeal; yellow cornmeal.

From left: Garlic bulb; garlic cloves; green onions; red onion.

CINNAMON STICK: dried aromatic inner bark of the shoots of the cinnamon tree. Used as a flavoring in sweet and savory dishes. Remove cinnamon sticks before serving.

Clockwise from left: Caraway seeds; cinnamon sticks; curry powder; mixed spice; paprika.

COARSE (KOSHER) SALT: a fairly coarse refined salt.

COCONUT:
Cream, unsweetened: available in cans and cartons in supermarkets and Asian stores; coconut milk can be substituted, although it is not as thick.
Milk, unsweetened: available in cans from supermarkets.

CORNMEAL: ground corn (maize), pale yellow and fine in texture. Yellow cornmeal cannot be substituted as the results will be different.

CORNMEAL, YELLOW: usually made from ground corn (maize); similar to cornmeal but coarser and darker in color. One cannot be substituted for the other.

CREAM:
Heavy: a cream that contains about 36 percent milkfat.
Sour: a thick commercially cultured soured cream.
Whipping: is specified when necessary in recipes.

CUMIN: a spice with a strong and distinctive aroma, like caraway, and a warm, spicy, aromatic and curry-like taste. Available in seed or ground form. Pictured on page 126.

CURRY POWDER: a convenient combination of powdered spices. It consists of ground chili peppers, coriander, cumin, fennel, fenugreek and turmeric in varying proportions.

FISH: we used white fish cutlets, fish steaks and firm boneless fish fillets. Choose your favorite variety.

FLOUR:
Self-rising: substitute all-purpose flour and double-acting baking powder in the proportions of 1 cup all-purpose flour to 2 level teaspoons of double-acting baking powder. Sift together several times before using.

GARLIC: can be used minced, sliced or in whole cloves; a bulb contains many cloves. Pictured above right. To mince garlic, see Techniques section.

GHEE: a pure butter fat available in supermarkets, it can be heated to high temperatures without burning because of the lack of salts and milk solids. You can make your own, if you prefer (see Techniques section).

GINGERROOT:
Fresh or green: scrape away outside skin and grate, chop or slice gingerroot as required. To preserve fresh, peeled gingerroot, cover with dry sherry in a jar and refrigerate.

Fresh gingerroot.

GOLDEN RAISINS: seedless white raisins.

GREEN ONIONS: also known as scallions. The white section and most of the green section are used. Pictured top.

HERBS: we have specified when to use fresh or dried herbs. We used dried (not ground) herbs in the proportions of 1:4 for fresh herbs; for example, 1 teaspoon dried herbs instead of 4 teaspoons chopped fresh herbs. For an easy way to chop fresh herbs, see Techniques section.

HERB AND GARLIC DRESSING: available in bottles from supermarkets.

HOISIN SAUCE: a thick, sweet Chinese barbeque sauce made from a mixture of salted black beans, onion and garlic.

HORSERADISH CREAM: a paste of horseradish, oil, mustard and flavorings.

LAMB:
Chops: choose sirloin, loin or rib chops.
Rack: row of chops. A rack can consist of 2 chops or more, as required.

LASAGNE NOODLES, NO-BOIL: require no pre-cooking. Available from supermarkets in white, whole-wheat and spinach varieties.

LEEK: a member of the onion family, resembles the green onion but is much larger. To prepare leeks, see Techniques section.

LENTILS: dried pulses. There are many different varieties, and they are usually identified and named after their color.

LETTUCE: we used mostly Boston and romaine lettuce in this book. Any lettuce can be used as a substitute.

MAYONNAISE: an emulsion sauce made with egg yolks, oil and vinegar or lemon juice.

MIXED SPICE: a mixture of ground spices usually consisting of cinnamon, allspice and nutmeg. Pictured page 126.

MUSHROOMS:
Button: small, unopened mushrooms with a delicate flavor.
Flat: large, soft, flat mushrooms which have a rich strong flavor.

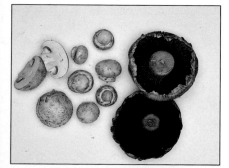

From left: Button mushrooms; flat mushrooms.

MUSTARD:
Dry: available in powder form.
Seeded: a French-style mustard with crushed mustard seeds.

NUTMEG: the dried nut of an evergreen tree native to Indonesia; it is available in ground and whole form or you can grate your own with a fine grater. Pictured page 126.

OIL:
Olive: virgin oil is obtained only from the pulp of high-grade fruit. Pure olive oil is pressed from the pulp and kernels of second-grade olives. Extra virgin olive oil is the purest quality virgin oil. Suitable for salad dressings and marinades.
Polyunsaturated vegetable: used for shallow and deep-frying.
Salad: used in dressings.

OYSTER-FLAVORED SAUCE: a rich brown sauce made from oysters cooked in salt and soy sauce, then thickened.

PAPPADAMS: made from lentils and sold in packages in different sizes.

PAPRIKA: made from ground dried peppers, and varying in taste from mild to hot and sweet. Pictured on page 124.

PARSLEY, FLAT-LEAFED: also known as Continental parsley or Italian parsley; the flavor is different from curled parsley.

From left: Curled parsley; flat-leafed parsley.

PEARL ONIONS: tiny onions used in pickles and casseroles.

PHYLLO PASTRY: a tissue-thin pastry bought chilled or frozen.

PITA POCKET: 2-layered flat breads, which can be cut open to form a pocket. They are an individual serving size of the large pita bread rounds.

PORK:
Leg cutlets: thin slices of pork.
Sliced pork belly: cut from the rib end of the belly.

PORT WINE: fortified wine.

POTATOES: use old potatoes unless otherwise specified.
Baby: very small new potatoes.

PUFF PASTRY, READY-ROLLED: frozen sheets of puff pastry available from supermarkets.

PUMPKIN SQUASH: there are several varieties; any type can be substituted for the other.

RED CURRANT JELLY: a preserve made from red currants; available from some supermarkets and delicatessens.

RICE:
Brown: natural whole-grain; takes longer to cook than white rice.
Jasmine: used extensively in Thai cooking. Has a unique delicate aroma and flavor.
White: is hulled and polished, can be short- or long-grained.

Clockwise from left: Short-grain rice; long-grain rice; jasmine rice.

RICE VERMICELLI: rice noodles.

SAFFRON: available in threads or ground form, made from the dried stamens of the crocus flower. Quality varies greatly.

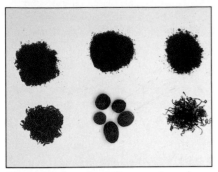

Clockwise from top left: ground cumin; ground nutmeg; ground saffron; saffron threads; whole nutmeg; cuminseeds.

SAMBAL OELEK:
(also ulek and olek): a paste made from ground chili peppers and salt.

SEASONED PEPPER: a combination of black pepper, sugar and bell peppers.

SNOW PEAS: also known as Chinese pea pods. Top and tail before steaming or blanching.

From left: Snow peas; sugar snap peas.

SOY SAUCE: made from fermented soy beans. The light sauce is generally used with white meat, and the darker variety with red meat. There is a multi-purpose salt-reduced sauce available; also Japanese soy sauce.

SPINACH: a soft-leaved vegetable, delicate in taste; young Swiss chard can be substituted for spinach. Pictured above right.

From top: Swiss chard; spinach.

SUGAR: we used coarse granulated table sugar unless otherwise specified.
Dark brown: a soft, fine granulated sugar with molasses present which gives characteristic color.
Superfine: fine granulated table sugar.

SUGAR SNAP PEAS: are small pods with small formed peas inside; they are eaten whole, cooked or uncooked. They require only a short cooking time. Pictured below left.

SWEET POTATO: we used an orange-colored sweet potato. White sweet potato is also available.

TAHINI (SESAME PASTE): made from crushed sesame seeds.

THREE-BEAN MIX: canned mixture of three varieties of beans; drain and rinse well before using. Any bean mix or canned beans could be substituted.

TOMATO:
Cherry tomatoes: small and round tomatoes, usually available all year.
Paste: a concentrated tomato puree used for flavoring soups, stews, sauces and casseroles, etc.

VEAL:
Cutlet: thinly sliced piece cut from the leg.
Rolled roast: cuts suitable for rolling are shoulder, breast and leg.
Steak: usually cut from the leg. Can be pan-fried or braised.

VINEGAR: we used both white and brown (malt) vinegar.
Cider: made from apples; has an acidic taste and smell.
Red wine: made from the fermentation of red grapes.

WINE: we used good-quality dry white and red wines.

WINE VINEGAR: made from wine, often flavored with herbs, spices and fruit, etc.

WORCESTERSHIRE SAUCE: a spicy sauce used mainly on red meat.

YOGURT: plain, unflavored yogurt is used as a meat tenderizer, enricher, thickener and also as a dessert ingredient.

ZEST: the finely grated peel of citrus fruit.

CUP AND SPOON MEASURES

To ensure accuracy in your recipes use standard metric measuring equipment.

(a) 8oz fluid cup for measuring liquids.

(b) a graduated set of four cups – measuring 1 cup, half, third and quarter cup – for items such as flour, sugar, etc. When measuring in these fractional cups, level off at the brim.

(c) a graduated set of five spoons: tablespoon (½ fluid oz liquid capacity), teaspoon, half, quarter and eighth teaspoons.

All our spoon measurements are level.

We have used large eggs with an average weight of 2oz each in all recipes.

INDEX

Home Library
Salads
Sensational recipes for all occasions

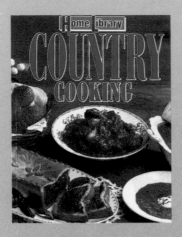

Home Library
COUNTRY
COOKING

Home Library
Healthy
Heart
Cookbook
LOWER
CHOLESTEROL
YOUR

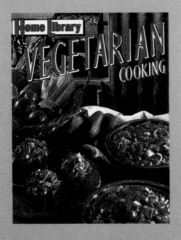

Home Library
VEGETARIAN COOKING

THE BEST
Home Library
SEAFOOD
RECIPES

Home Library
Italian
COOKING CLASS
COOKBOOK

Home Library
CHICKEN
COOKBOOK
PLUS duck, quail, turkey, goose and more

Home Library
PASTA
COOKBOOK
More than 170 recipes

Home Library
CHINESE
COOKING CLASS
COOKBOOK

Home Library
STARTERS
AND
SOUPS

Home Library
BEGINNERS

Home Library
FINGER FOOD
Best ever party food
Tempting hot and cold savouries
Do ahead and freezing tips